Writings
ON THE NILE

By the same author

Samuel Daniel. A Critical and Biographical Study
Ed. *Daniel's The Vision of the Twelve Goddesses* in *A Book of Masques*
Fulke Greville, Lord Brooke
Selections from the works of Fulke Greville
Shakespeare and the Story
The Poetry of Dante Gabriel Rossetti
Sir Philip Sidney and 'Arcadia'

Writings
ON THE NILE

Harriet Martineau
Florence Nightingale
Amelia Edwards

Joan Rees

 THE RUBICON PRESS

The Rubicon Press
57 Cornwall Gardens
London SW7 4BE

British Library Cataloguing-in-Publication Data.

A catalogue record for this book is available from the British Library.

0-948695-39-0 (hardback edition)
0-948695-40-4 (paperback edition)

Printed and bound in Great Britain by Biddles Limited of Guildford
and King's Lynn

Contents

List of Illustrations

For David and Elin

Acknowledgements

I gratefully acknowledge the following: The Mathaf Gallery for permission to reproduce "A Street in Cairo" by John Varley; the Principal and Fellows of Somerville College, Oxford, for permission to reproduce the portrait of Amelia Edwards and to consult their Amelia Edwards papers; the Egypt Exploration Society for permission to consult their archives; the National Portrait Gallery for permission to reproduce the portraits of Harriet Martineau, Florence Nightingale and Lucie Duff Gordon; Mr Peter A. Clayton for his kindly interest and advice; and, in particular, Mr Martin Davies, FSA, to whom I am indebted for invaluable assistance.

Responsibility for the text, and any errors, omissions or other deficiencies which may be found in it, rests with the author alone.

Preface

This is not a book about Egypt but about reactions to Egypt and, more particularly, to ancient Egypt. At its centre is a study of three women of middle-class English background who separately travelled there in the nineteenth century, Harriet Martineau in 1846, Florence Nightingale in 1849, and Amelia Edwards in 1873. Each of them wrote an account of her experiences; Harriet Martineau and Amelia Edwards, both professional writers, devoted books to their journeys and what became of them, Florence Nightingale wrote letters home which were later privately printed and in 1987 became available in a selected edition.

The opening up of Egypt following Napoleon's invasion stimulated many travellers and many travellers' tales. Some were drawn to make the journey because of the connections with Biblical history - one of the principal incentives to exploration and excavation in early days was the prospect of finding evidences of Biblical figures and events; some welcomed the challenge of unfamiliar territory and peoples as an adventure to be undertaken with dash and vigour; some, especially in the later years of the century, went because it had become the smart thing to do; many were moved, whether before they set out or in the course of their stay, by the revelation of an ancient past which opened up dimensions of thought they had previously not known. Harriet Martineau, Florence Nightingale and Amelia Edwards acknowledge with more or less sympathy all these motivations but they themselves belong pre-eminently to the last class and their books explore more fully and more evocatively than any other what was involved and implied in their century's encounter with ancient Egypt. What they have to say leads back time and again to the situations and preoccupations of their own time and country and in so doing sheds light from a new angle on nineteenth century life and thought. They also bear witness to the powerful effect which Egypt had and continues to have on the individual mind and imagination: twentieth century travellers on the Nile may find in these books an eloquent formulation of their own less articulate reactions.

Egyptological research has progressed far beyond even what it was in Amelia Edwards's time and books about Egypt proliferate year by year. More significantly from the present point of view, writers continue to set their fictions in Egypt, finding there a special resonance and an impulse to lift accustomed horizons. "To any vision must be brought an eye adapted to what is to be seen", as Plotinus wrote, words quoted by E.M. Forster as an epigraph to his guide to Alexandria, but eyes have been opened in Egypt to perceive vistas to which they were blind before. Harriet Martineau, Florence Nightingale and Amelia Edwards stand at the centre of this process. Each by the experiences of her previous life and her particular mental and temperamental cast brought an eye adapted to what was to be seen but each also demonstrates that Plotinus' adage does not tell the whole truth. What is to be seen itself varies according to the nature of the beholder and the three women all saw something different, found it deeply and personally significant and acknowledged that it had a profound and lasting effect on their lives. The impact of Egypt on Harriet Martineau, Florence Nightingale and Amelia Edwards is a matter of social, religious and personal history all combining with the imaginative stimulus of Egypt to produce a particular ferment, individual to them but relevant and effective in other minds also.

These women possessed strong minds, physical courage and stamina and, above all, each felt a compelling need to pursue an active career. They did not have today's option of combining a career with marriage and for each of them, when choice had to be made, the drive towards free and independent action was stronger than any other competing urge. Harriet Martineau and Amelia Edwards were keenly aware of the struggle it was for any of their sex to be accepted as fully competent and mature individuals but they themselves succeeded in establishing prominent positions in hitherto masculine territory. Florence Nightingale, for her part, took on the government and the medical establishment and changed not only the status of nursing but also that of the British common soldier. Some kinds of personal fulfilment were forfeited in the process but others were achieved: all three were fortunate in being able to choose what was to be sacrificed and what was to be nurtured. The key to choice lay, in the first place, in their gifts but, for Harriet Martineau and Amelia Edwards, also in the fact that straitened family circumstances put them under pressure to become income earners. Florence Nightingale, on the other hand, was shackled by affluence, forced by a well-to-do family into dependence and conformity with social obligations which maddened her. It needed a war to release her from this thraldom. As a result of the intensity of her struggle, she developed a fierce, even ferocious singleness of purpose, by comparison with which Harriet Martineau, dedicated as she always was, seems almost a waverer. The work she saw to be done was too urgent to leave any time or patience for talk of women's rights and female suffrage. What was wanted was less talk and more willingness to undertake hard work. She had nothing but contempt for "ladies" who came out to the Crimea, ostensibly to help in the hospitals, but who shrank from the unsavoury and physically demanding tasks which were actually required to be done. Though she dismissed campaigns and causes as an irrelevance, her career, like those of the others, was a powerful witness to the major contribution women could make to public life. Harriet Martineau, in particular, claimed a prominent public role and filled it with energy and distinction for many years.

What follows will be a study of the impact of Egypt, with Harriet Martineau's *Eastern Life Present and Past*, Florence Nightingale's *Letters from Egypt* and Amelia Edwards's *A Thousand Miles up the Nile* as key texts. The introductory chapter will provide a brief general context, both historical and literary. The following chapters devoted to individual authors will give biographical sketches and also consider some of their work apart from the Egyptian books. Writing was the means by which Harriet Martineau and Amelia Edwards earned their living and samples of their fiction contribute valuably to our understanding of the kinds of mind and imagination which they brought to bear on their Egyptian experiences. Florence Nightingale did not earn her living by her pen but it was her principal weapon in the battle she fought to improve standards of nursing and hospital management. She wrote copiously and trenchantly, mostly letters and reports, but she also wrote the passionate and personal *Cassandra*, an attack on the restrictions imposed on women of her class by her society. *Cassandra* is a vital document in any appreciation of Florence Nightingale and no less an indispensable part of the background to her Egyptian letters.

It was ancient Egypt which stimulated these women and which dominates their narratives but another woman's record of Egyptian experience is strikingly different. Lucie Duff Gordon went to Egypt in 1862 in search of health. She lived there, mainly in Luxor, for seven years and the Egypt that concerned her was that of the present and the lives which interested her were those of the people she lived among, not the Pharaohs and fellaheen of a long-distant past. She felt the impact of Egypt no less than others though the impression it made took different form. Her testimony to what it meant to her helps to fill out the picture of English responses to "the East" in the nineteenth century and it is noted in the final chapter as a piquant contrast to those of her three contemporaries. Harriet Martineau, Florence Nightingale and Amelia Edwards observed and commented on the living world of modern Egypt but they were never a part of that world as Lucie Duff Gordon was. The Egypt that she writes of is in effect a different country from theirs.

This book in its main emphasis is offered as a tribute to the three remarkable women who are its principal subjects, as a contribution to knowledge of the nineteenth century and also as the record of a phenomenon with far-reaching ramifications in both the nineteenth and twentieth centuries: that is the psychological, philosophical and spiritual impact on modern consciousness of the rediscovery of ancient Egypt.

Introduction

Thou, silent form, dost tease us out of thought
As doth eternity
(*Keats*)

(i)

Visitors to Egypt throughout the centuries have been staggered by the sight of the ancient buildings, the statues, the carvings, the paintings, all visible evidence of a long-gone but vibrant past. More than half obliterated by sand though they have been, built over by mud huts, defaced or denuded by the uncaring or hostile hands of later generations, in spite of all it has never been possible to be indifferent to these witnesses to life long ago. From Cairo to Aswan, and through Nubia too till the building of the High Dam, the Nile carries on its banks, like an unwinding scroll, the evidence of an advanced and confident civilization in a past so remote that it makes the classical world seem modern. Now, after the hiatus of Lake Nasser, Abu Simbel stands as a final, breath-stopping image. Twentieth century politics and engineering have added their quota of change to ancient Egypt but have not removed the temples' power to overwhelm: the tombs shake the balance of thought even more dramatically and disturbingly. Egypt is in a sense familiar now, package tour territory with travel agencies competing for custom and offering every modern amenity to protect visitors from too rude an encounter with the unfamiliar and discomfiting. Even so, dull of soul indeed must be the man or woman who can enter the tombs without feeling a shiver - not of cold, for the tombs are warm - but of deep feelings stirred, however transiently and however little or inadequately defined.

Two impressions dominate. One is the dramatic collision produced by the known age of these places where the long-gone dead were laid and the effect of immediate still-urgent life created by the reliefs and the paintings which decorate them. Even today, the colours of some are still bright and clear as if they had just been

1

laid on. Time has not diminished the force of feeling embodied in the scenes of gods and goddesses, pharaohs and nobles and their consorts, receiving and bestowing blessings and gifts. In those tombs where scenes of everyday life are depicted rather than religious themes, the sense of active, breathing people living their lives in the here and now is almost dazzling. In the tombs of Egypt Hardy's image from *A Pair of Blue Eyes*, "Time folded up like a fan before him", acquires a new potency. Hardy's hero, Knight, hangs from a cliff-face, in danger of falling at any moment to his death and, his nerves keyed to hyper-awareness at this crisis, sees near him a fossil, the remains of a creature that once lived as he does and, unknown ages ago, died as he is about to do. His meditation on time, given his circumstances, is slightly preposterous in the novel; but the swish and snap of that closing fan, that sudden obliteration of intervening ages as centuries vanish within its folds, are almost audible in the silence of an Egyptian tomb. Time collapses and the poise of even the most sophisticated is shaken.

The western mind is further bewildered by a second powerful impression: the tombs violate most flagrantly what is generally taken to be an inbuilt principle of human behaviour. To contemplate, however slightly, the technical skill, the artistry, the intellectual organization of the tomb decorations, is to be baffled by the mind-processes through which so much endeavour was devoted to work which it was intended no-one should ever see. The workman was worthy of his hire but he was denied what may be thought a right without which the work loses its savour: the admiration and applause of his own time and of posterity. Nevertheless he laboured with all the skill he had until the tomb was sealed, for ever as he thought. Now, three or four thousand years later, these things are at last seen but whether the craftsmen and artists would be pleased is doubtful. If gratified by the recognition and praise, they might yet balance this pleasure against a terrible sense of loss.

The tombs, in fact, speak to us of time and of life and death and our minds receive their message as questions: what is time? what is life, what is death? which is which? The Egyptian workman did not think that his work would never be looked at. He laboured for those who would live again in the other life beyond death and for the gods who demanded and appreciated the best he could give.

2

The audience he expected was wider and infinitely more exalted than any number of scholars or art connoisseurs or casual gazers could ever be. Our shock at time's fan suddenly closing and our troubled incomprehension of the artists' motivation measure the impact that Egypt can make on even travel-hardened and over-exposed late twentieth century minds.

Nineteenth century travellers were in some ways different but not essentially so. A major distinction in their situation was that Egypt and its monuments came to them as a new revelation. In 1798 the young Napoleon, seeking new worlds to conquer, had landed near Alexandria and successfully fought off the Turks. In the next three years, though the French navy was crushingly defeated by Nelson and the army cut off, his troops were to penetrate far down the Nile. He had seen himself as another Alexander, but his sense of history extended further than that. Two months after landing he exhorted his soldiers to battle by rousing their consciousness of the great stage they acted on: "Soldats!" he cried, "du haut de ces pyramides quarante siècles vous contemplent!" It was quite in character that he should have brought with his army one hundred and sixty seven scientists and technicians, including a number of scholars eminent in the disciplines of the time and, at least as important, sixteen cartographers and surveyors. Napoleon's army and its followers were to discover and to study Egypt as well as to occupy it. The military adventure was ended by the British at the battle of Alexandria in March 1801 but the influence of French occupation was long-lasting and the influence of the *savants* who travelled with the army even more so. For the first time Egyptian antiquities were subjected to serious and systematic study and a dynasty of French scholars was founded. These were to be in the forefront of the new science of Egyptology which gained momentum throughout the century. To go to Egypt in the first half of the nineteenth century was to go to a country which was at the same time old and yet also new. Many of its wonders had been freshly and excitingly revealed by the great Belzoni and others who followed on the heels of the French yet many secrets remained buried below centuries of accretions of sand and the rubbish of the ages. Visitors walking to inspect some site might find their feet caught in mummy cloths and kicking the arms and legs or even heads of shrivelled and dismembered corpses. They might also come across, by chance, a previously unknown rock temple or tomb and there was ample opportunity to acquire and carry home some rare memento, a mummy case, for example, or the mummy itself, a stone sarcophagus or a piece of statuary. Travelling could be rough and the monuments themselves were neglected, many of them built over or obscured by sand; but counterbalancing these disadvantages was the sense of first-hand contact with a world just emerged from centuries of oblivion, and of being among the first to look upon scenes and objects that no eye had seen for a thousand years or even, perhaps, for far longer. It was possible to take time, to take days or weeks exploring a major site, to become imbued with its atmosphere, to become totally familiar with the topography. As always, the depth of the impact these things made depended on the nature of the receiving mind.

In so far as industrious study could make them so, many Victorians were well prepared for Egypt. The travelling classes possessed, as part of their educational background, an intimate knowledge of the Bible and a familiarity with the Egypt of Biblical history. This was not an unqualified advantage for what they thought they knew from the Biblical source was often misleading or false; but nevertheless it gave them some historical background. Beyond this, there was much else to assimilate. The reading lists given in Murray's 1873 *Handbook for Rome* contained some forty titles, most of them multi-volume works in German, Italian, or French.[1] Egypt had not accumulated such a bulk but Egyptian travellers shared their classical compatriots' redoubtable capacity for digesting informative works. A number of substantial books were already in existence and had to be conscientiously studied both beforehand and on voyage. Before the advent of Cook's steamers, flat-bottomed boats called dahabiehs were used for Nile travel. They possessed many amenities but the journey was slow and there were long hours available in which to learn by heart the order of the dynasties and study all that was known about the next site to be visited. Florence Nightingale's bibliography, which includes works by Belzoni, Bruce, Bunsen, Champollion, Lane, Lepsius and Wilkinson, is not untypical.[2]

4

If provision for stocking up the mind was an essential part of preparations, so also was the accumulation of a vast number of objects intended to ensure the physical well-being of the traveller. The lists of medical items, stores, recommended clothing and other equipment offered for the guidance of the traveller in Egypt are at least as daunting as the reading requirements.[3] Very highly recommended was a Levinge, a sort of sleeping bag-cum-mosquito net into which the body was inserted and which was then laced up tightly. The hope, not always realized, was that fleas, flies and other bugs would be thwarted by this fortification and the traveller, swathed rather like a mummy and weary after a hard day's sightseeing, would pass the night unmolested.

The fearsome Levinge is just one indication that travel on the Nile in the early years required fortitude and resolution as well as, ideally, intellectual stamina. Dahabiehs were commonly sunk before a party embarked for a voyage so as to drown the rats and other vermin which were lodged in them but this did not prevent the journey itself being a constant fight against small and vicious predators. The severity of the laws enacted by Muhammad Ali against any interference with foreigners meant that serious hostility from the natives was not likely but, all the same, precautions had to be taken, and trouble occasionally arose. By the later years of the century, much had improved but by then it was less intellectual curiosity or a spirit of adventure which took the British to the Nile than a compulsion to be in the fashion. A kind of Egyptian fever took hold for some years producing, among other things, the Egyptian Hall in Piccadilly and Egyptian Avenue in Highgate Cemetery. It was responsible for severe social embarrassment on at least one occasion when no fewer than three Cleopatras, to their mutual annoyance, attended the fancy dress ball given by the Duchess of Devonshire in 1897 to celebrate Queen Victoria's Diamond Jubilee. The provinces also succumbed to the infection. Writing of Ashton-under-Lyne in the last decades of the century, the much-admired *Manchester Guardian* journalist, William Haslam Mills, noted "a fearful, outbreak of Egyptology" in the neighbourhood: Ashton families and their connections were, in fact, prominent supporters of Egyptian research and conservation.[4]

Cook's handbook for 1875-76, *Up the Nile by Steam*, fully acknowledges that Egypt and the Nile represented high fashion and makes no bones about the company's desire to break the hold of the dahabiehs on the modish imagination. Cook's had introduced steamer cruises in 1869 and were vigorous in promoting their initiative by deriding the supposed attractions of the private boat. "Nothing has probably been so fully described and praised to exhaustion as the famous Dahabeah", the handbook remarks sarcastically, "and the idyllic charms of life in one of these boats, floating up and down the Nile, have been sung in every imaginable strain. No doubt, for a party of very dear friends on a shooting excursion, a young couple on their honeymoon, invalids in search of health, young swells who have nothing at all to do on earth but kill time and throw away their money - in fact, for any one who can easily shut himself out from all communication with the civilised world, and has got the temper to lie idle for weeks and months, looking every day on the same uniformly desolate scenery - nothing can be more delicious..." This is strong stuff but, in spite of the fighting talk, Cook's themselves organized some dahabieh parties in the 1870s. In the long run steamers won the day and the diatribe of 1875, for all its prejudice, makes it easy to see why. There were, as the booklet points out, great disadvantages to the dahabiehs, among them the possibility of serious accidents when boats capsized, the recurrent and frustrating delays as the wind was either too strong or too weak for sailing, and the difficulty, if not impossibility, of getting prompt attention in case of illness or other emergencies on board. It is as well, when envying the early travellers for their more leisurely progress through the sites, to bear in mind the tedium and worse disabilities which accompanied it.

The journey, however accomplished and for whatever purpose, left its impress on many. How many letters home, remarkable for nothing but the dutifulness of the correspondents, how many diaries for which immortality was hoped but never attained, how many accounts which saw print but have long since been forgotten - like the song the sirens sang, the full extent of writing on Egypt in the nineteenth century is unknowable. Some books and some travellers were and remain notable, not all of them reverential. Kinglake's *Eothen*, for example, first published in 1844, owes much to its author's promise that it will be "quite superficial in its character". Egypt was only part of his itinerary when in 1834, at the age of twenty-five, he embarked on a journey through the Middle East. He made no pretence to the erudition and conscientious assembling of fact which travellers and travel book writers generally regarded as their duty but, on the contrary, he blithely discarded all that. "I believe I may truly acknowledge," he wrote in his Preface, "that from all details of geographical discovery, or antiquarian research - from all display of 'sound learning and religious knowledge' - from all historical and scientific illustrations - from all useful statistics - from all political disquisitions - and from all good moral reflections, the volume is thoroughly free."[5] The book is lively and quirky and gave contemporary readers great relief from the more ponderous and pompous lucubrations of others. In the late twentieth century, however, its appeal diminishes. Kinglake writes of all he sees and all whom he meets with an unshakeable confidence in "the natural ascendancy of Europeans" (p. 236) and he takes occasion to note his displeasure at observing that even Englishmen may sometimes be influenced by other peoples' minds. Fortunately, he adds, "their good sense and sound religious knowledge would be likely to guard them from error" (p.100). The particular error and pernicious alien influence which he deplores concerns "magic", or any sense of the supernatural or the numinous which is not accredited by Reason, the English deity. Given these attitudes, it is not to be expected that he would be moved by the neglected Egyptian temples but one monument does impress him. The Great Pyramid, ancient and immense as it was, could not be ignored and it even stirred in him, from deep in the subconscious, powerful and unanalysable feelings. "...the remoteness of its origin, no less than the enormity of its proportions - screens an Egyptian Pyramid from the easy and familiar contact of our modern minds", he writes in uncharacteristic vein. He quickly recovers his assurance: "the Pyramids are quite of this world; ...they were piled up into the air for the realization of some kingly crotchets about immortality, some priestly longing for burial fees; and...they were built like coral rocks by swarms of insects - by swarms of poor Egyptians, who were not only the abject tools and slaves of power, but who also ate onions for the reward of their immortal labours!" (p.214) The onions, a detail derived from Herodotus, serve safely to inoculate the English gentleman against any passing inclination to take seriously either the kingly aspirations to immortality, or the priests who officiated at the ceremonies, or the poor Egyptians or, indeed, the society which produced them all.

"My excuse for the book is its truth", Kinglake claimed (p.xix). He wrote about what had interested him at the time and what he had felt, regardless of whether or not it corresponded with conventional expectations. The popularity his book came to enjoy was his justification but he would not have been so popular if he had been truly eccentric. His tastes and his responses to his experiences reflect the society he came from and flatter it. It was interesting and adventurous to travel in the Middle East and see exotic sights and meet strange people who were so very un-English. At home people were avid to read these tales of dragomen and bedouins and thrill to descriptions of the "sad, earnest" eyes of the Sphinx and the everlasting tranquillity of its mien (p.217); but in all this there was nothing unsettling, only stimulus for the romantic imagination, *Eothen* was very successful in its day. Time and different attitudes have exposed its flaws, none more glaring than the over-heating which occurs whenever Kinglake writes, as he often does, of women. His fantasies are of timidity and surrender with occasional role-reversal when he thrills himself with imaginary self-abasement before some imperious beauty whom he glimpses in a window and whom he endows with "fierceness...pride, passion, and power" (p.56). It was not likely that he would have resisted the slave markets and the harems.

They were, in fact, a regular part of the tourist programme and Kinglake took some pains in Cairo to get a sight of white women for sale. That he had "not the least notion of purchasing" makes this less, rather than more excusable, for it exposes him to a charge of prurient curiosity. The one white girl he succeeded in seeing was very young but also very fat and he did not conceal his "distaste and disappointment" (pp.199-200). As he had written earlier: "It is a great shame, but the truth is that, except when we refer to the beautiful devotion of the mother to her child, all the

8

fine things we say and think about women apply only to those who are tolerably good-looking or graceful" (p.166) . It was natural, in the circumstances, that a visit to a harem offended his taste not his conscience. His host made his two wives bundle out before Kinglake was admitted but this, he suspected, was less from jealousy than a fear that neither of them would stand up to his discriminating judgement. Fastidiously assessing the décor of the rooms, Kinglake decided that his host was right: "One is apt to judge of a woman before one sees her by the air of elegance or coarseness with which she surrounds her home. I judged Osman's wives by this test, and condemned them both." (p.188)

Eliot Warburton was a traveller with much in common with Kinglake, in outlook if not in life. Warburton was the son of an Irish Inspector General of Police, educated at Cambridge and called to the Irish Bar. He had a taste for adventure and met a premature death in 1851 on one of his excursions. His book, *The Crescent and the Cross*, also published in 1844, does not have the literary qualities of *Eothen*, with the consequence that essentially similar underlying attitudes stand out the more starkly. Warburton had a robust, no-nonsense approach to the lesser breeds of the Middle East: "A brace of pistols in one's girdle, and kurbash, or hippopotamus-whip in one's hand, does more in the East towards the promotion of courtesy, good-humour, and good fellowship, than all the smiles and eloquence that ever were exerted" (p.82). His mode is a mixture of the swash-buckling, Boys' Own paper derring-do and the sentimentally romantic and, as with Kinglake, his response to women exposes the pressures and repressions and fantasies of his time and background. He too visits slave markets and, less concerned with the niceties of interior decoration than Kinglake, he writes with tender enthusiasm of the life of the harem women: "Born and brought up in the hareem, women never seem to pine at its imprisonment: like cage-born birds, they sing among their bars, and discover in their aviaries a thousand little pleasures invisible to eyes that have a wider range. To them in their calm seclusion, the strifes of the battling world come softened and almost hushed; they only hear the far-off murmur of life's stormy sea; and, if their human lot dooms them to their cares, they are as transient as those of childhood" (pp.42-3). It is clear enough that he finds in this rosy vision of harem life the perfect realization of the nineteenth century Englishman's dream of the innocent child-wife, protected in impossible purity from every contaminating experience.[6] The sadistic element in the psychological tangle involved here is made apparent when he immediately follows his praise of the harem by recounting with relish the story of one "poor Fatima" who aroused the jealousy of her lord and was duly consigned to the waters of the Nile.

Like Kinglake, Warburton is not a man to be much impressed by relics of an ancient and alien civilization. His experience of the pyramids is dominated by the behaviour of the bedouin guides and his account is a celebration of the efficacy of pistols, kicks, and threats of the bastinado; but, as happened to Kinglake, one sight in Egypt does penetrate beneath the skin. He is impressed by Thebes. It was "with astonishment, and almost with awe", he writes, (p.157), that he rode through the ruins of that once mighty city. "The world contains nothing like it" (p.158) and the impression, he believes, will remain with him for ever.[7] These are striking reactions from a man who is not naturally sympathetic to Egypt or to Egyptians and who has certainly not bothered to prepare himself to appreciate the ancient remains. Travel did not then necessarily broaden the mind, any more than it does now, and it is comforting to know that two such determined British imperialists as Kinglake and Warburton were capable of being moved, at least occasionally, out of their characteristic unimpressability.

These are travellers' tales of the first half of the nineteenth century, lively records of the responses of cultivated men from northern islands to the past and the present of Egypt. Neither Kinglake nor Warburton attempts to be edifyingly instructive or informative but they are all the more revealing about the habits of mind and preconceptions of their countrymen in their encounters with the uncompromisingly different life of the Middle East. They travelled rough in circumstances very different from those of their successors in later decades who cruised at leisure on the Nile, expecting and often receiving every home comfort, frequently including, among other refinements, a piano. In February, 1854, on the island of Philae, Edward Lear feasted nobly one evening on macaroni, turkey, rock pigeons and pancakes[8] and it was not uncommon for plum puddings to be served on Christmas Day. Marianne North, famous naturalist and friend of Amelia Edwards, records meeting a couple who were having problems in finding a dahabieh large enough to hold them, their servants and "huge packages from Fortnum and Mason's". The lady was at the same time looking for a second maid as the one she had was delicate and often unable to rise to the exertion of doing her mistress's hair![9]. Not all Nile travellers in the later part of the century are likely to have had quite the same sense of life's necessities but this pair, accustomed to being waited on hand and foot and secure in the belief that it was their right, as members of a dominant society, to expect and demand every privilege, were not untypical. The imperialist strain grew stronger throughout the century. Some were more sensitive than Kinglake and Warburton to what they saw and many were better informed but these two had their share in preparing the way for the development of Egyptian travel in both its good and bad aspects. They appealed to the imagination of the general public in a way that more sober tomes could not and aroused curiosity and excitement about the lands they travelled in. Egypt with its Sphinx and its pyramids, its temples and its tombs was a land to be visited and on the journey somewhere, a view, a ruined pylon or a group of pillars might open a sudden prospect of a world where the familiar writ did not run but which nevertheless roused feelings of awe and even, perhaps, a kind of affinity.

Harriet Martineau, Florence Nightingale and Amelia Edwards touched on deeper issues than the men. They also, on the whole, took a more genial view of native character. Their attitudes range from Harriet Martineau's sympathetic understanding of what the noise of the sakia meant to a poor Egyptian peasant,[10] through Amelia Edwards's more detached goodwill, to the revulsion which Florence Nightingale expresses at the debased condition of many of the poor. Protected as they were by dragomen, boat crews and other escorts, the situation of these women was, of course, very different from that of adventure-seekers like Kinglake and Warburton. Their relative immunity to harassment had the advantage of enabling them to observe individuals from another angle and to note different things but the contrast between their responses to Egypt and those of typical male contemporaries cannot be entirely

11

explained by this. Without the classical education which men of their station received, they were less likely to take their standards from Greece and Rome and were, perhaps, for that reason correspondingly more susceptible to the impact of another ancient civilization. The keen and sympathetic interest which each of them took in ancient Egyptian religion may have owed something to grateful recognition of less fierce and repressive deities than the patriarchal god preached in English churches. Each of them, moreover, came to Egypt highly charged with intellectual and other energies for which women did not find an easy outlet in Victorian England. Egypt touched chords in each of them which vibrated profoundly and their books, consequently, have a depth and complexity of interest which the men's do not match. This last point will emerge prominently in the chapters which follow.

(ii)

Numerous as are the accounts of travel in Egypt in the nineteenth century, it is a striking and puzzling fact that none of the major poets or novelists was inspired either by the rediscovery of the ancient kingdom or the new visibility of the country. Shelley might be counted an exception but his "Ozymandias" is essentially a shot in a political crusade with little relevance to the statue of Rameses II which is its ostensible subject. The arrival in the British Museum of a statue of a winged beast from Nineveh moved Rossetti to reflect on the endurance of a sculpture and the evanescence of the generations of men who had lived beneath its shadow. He plays with the idea that among the Egyptian mummies also in the museum there might be some who in their lives knew Nineveh in its heyday:

> And now, - they and their gods and thou
> All relics here together, - now
> Whose profit? whether bull or cow,
> Isis or Ibis, who or how,
> Whether of Thebes or Nineveh?[11]

The passing of faiths and of civilisations is a theme that Egypt was conspicuously well qualified to evoke but no great writer took it up. Artists, on the other hand, enthusiastically welcomed the exciting opportunities offered by the monuments, the landscapes and the exotica of Eastern life, David Roberts, Alma Tadema and Edward Lear among them. It is all the more remarkable that there is no corresponding literary response.

In the twentieth century, however, Egypt and its monuments have attracted novelists with widely different styles and purposes. Lawrence Durrell chose Alexandria as the setting for his *Quartet* and Agatha Christie made use of the atmosphere and associations of the Nile for one of her most popular books. *Death on the Nile* is a resonant title, capitalising on Egyptian preoccupation with death, and the setting gives to the familiar formula of murder and detection a special aura. "You know, I'm not much of a fellow for temples and sight-seeing and all that, but a place like this sort of gets you, if you know what I mean. Those old Pharaohs must have been wonderful fellows". So, through Simon Doyle, the mystery of ancient Egypt is mediated to a mass readership. Cornelia Robson adds a philosophic dimension. Outside the temples at Abu Simbel she remarks that "looking at them makes one feel so small - and rather like an insect - and that nothing matters very much really does it?". John Fowles in his *Daniel Martin*, a book with greater pretensions than *Death on the Nile*, also avails himself of the particular power of Egypt to set up mysterious vibrations. His hero takes his sexual and philosophic confusions up the Nile and finds that, though he begins by classing the Pharaohs with modern dictators, the ancient world is not to be so easily dismissed. It penetrates the skin of his modern rationality and gives him both destructive and enhancing experiences. It plays its part in enabling him eventually to re-establish his life.

Two recent examples of writing on Egypt are of special interest inasmuch as they reflect the particular attitudes and preoccupations of the late twentieth century as *Eothen* and *The Crescent and the Cross* do of the mid-nineteenth. William Golding's tale, "The Scorpion God"[12] is at first sight summarizable as an ironic and deflationary account of the ancient Egyptian emphasis on death and the ancient people's response to it. The story tells of a predynastic Pharaoh who, growing old, has lost his strength and his sexual potency and so, according to the custom of the time and place, he must accept that his time has come to die. It is equally taken for granted that his personal servants must follow him into his tomb and die with him. The young man known as the Liar is a highly prized companion of the Pharaoh because he amuses him with his power to spin stories (hence his title) and, precisely because of his indispensability, he also must certainly die with his master. The Liar, however, is far from accepting the necessity of this. He has gone so far outside traditional mental boundaries as to conceive of a quite different view of life and death. He refuses to accept death as an entry to a better world and clings instead to the here and now. In his desperation he blurts out a devastating rejection of his society and all it lives and dies by: "A patch of land no bigger than a farm - a handful of apes left high and dry by the tide of men - too ignorant, too complacent, too dim-witted to believe the world is more than ten miles of river - ...". The only life he believes in is the one he knows; the only value he accepts is survival. His is the point of view of the sceptical modern man rejecting (like Kinglake) the "magic" of a credulous people. Golding handles this confrontation between ancient and modern, or perhaps more truly between east and west, with great energy and wit. The Liar triumphs and ancient Egypt and its beliefs appear to be conclusively dismissed.

If this were all, it would be a reaction of a kind to the impact of Egypt. The story could be read as expressing an impatience with faddish, modern over-attention to ancient, rightly discarded ways of thinking, and deriding the folly of those who allow, what Kinglake (again) in his day found shocking among his compatriots, too much influence from other minds without submitting it to correction by a superior enlightenment. The story is, in fact, more subtle than that. The Liar is undoubtedly intelligent but in the face of death he is a hollow man, ignominious and unscrupulous, not hesitating to sacrifice another to save his own skin. The Pharaoh and his servants, by contrast, living by what the Liar dismisses as a derisory creed, go to death with dignity and joy, looking on it as a consummation most sincerely to be wished, a fulfilment not an extinction of life. The Liar triumphs and will assume the role and godhead of a Pharaoh. He will be the scorpion god and his scorpion sting will bleed the life out of the old civilization as,

14

stinging "like a scorpion", he has already killed the Head Man, chief guardian of the old ways.[13] "He has a death wish", the Head Man says before he dies, a remark left ambiguous, though what has gone before suggests a meaning. Early episodes in the story show the scorching heat of Pharaonic Egypt draining away vital energy and making passivity desirable. The imagined white men of the Liar's stories live in a cold climate and are active. They "dance at first" but after a while the cold overcomes them, just as heat overcomes the Egyptians, and turns them to stone. Lawrence gave a similar fate to Gerald Crich in *Women in Love* with a similar emblematic intention. Golding's story does not press readers to conclude that one way is wiser or more desirable than the other, the uncritical irrationality of the Egyptians or the insistent rationality of the modern west. The two are set in dynamic opposition. At least the source of the stimulus for this confrontation is clear. Whether the ancient Egyptian view of life and death exasperates or impresses, it is not easy to ignore it and the pull between contrary reactions creates the effective tension and drama of Golding's story.

Life and death and the nature of each are topics which the experience of Egypt presses insistently into the forefront of consciousness. They are at the heart of Golding's story as they are also of Janice Elliott's novel, *Life on the Nile*.[14] In this book another generation of tourists is cruising the Nile, a group of people brought together for reasons not fully explained, by a host whose character and career are also left in doubt. Charlotte Hamp is accompanying her husband, Leo, a travel writer, primarily because she wishes to find out more about her great-aunt, Phoebe, who had gone to Egypt as a young woman and been murdered there in mysterious circumstances. As she reads and re-reads the letters which Phoebe sent home and the journals she kept until moments before her death, Charlotte begins more and more to identify herself with her great-aunt and to find that past and present cross and interpenetrate in increasingly complex patterns. Mysterious and shadowy figures whose identity and rôle are never clear to Charlotte cross her path as they did Phoebe's and she becomes aware of many kinds of obscurity. This is not a voyage into a heart of darkness in Conrad's sense but it does take

Charlotte into a country of doubtful outlines, where people and events and experiences elude definition and refuse to be pinned down and categorized. The book could well have been entitled *Passage to Egypt* by analogy with Forster's novel. Forster's book is echoed several times in *Life on the Nile*, itself a structure of echoes as *Passage to India* is. Like Forster, Janice Elliott confronts a group of westerners with an ancient society which attracts the more sensitive amongst them at the same time as it baffles and frightens. It shakes them up or disorients them but if they are capable of sustaining the experience it enlarges them: "We lead these little, self-engrossed lives", Charlotte says towards the end of the novel. "But they're so fragile. Then there's a shock. It needn't be Egypt. I think in a funny way I'm glad I had that shock." (p.158)

As she says, it needn't be Egypt. Adela Quested might well have made Charlotte's comment and many books and many travellers testify to India's power to "shock"; but Egypt has its special qualifications as *Life on the Nile* effectively though obliquely conveys. The title contrasts directly with Agatha Christie's *Death on the Nile* although it is, in common terms, death rather than life which is the dominant theme. The novel has little to say about the great relics of the past but awareness of the powerful concentration on death as an inspiration of ancient Egyptian art underlies the several strands of the story. The second dominant theme is that quintessential concern of all who respond to the Egyptian experience: time. The temples and tombs of Egypt bring all who visit them face to face with an ancient past which is overwhelmingly real and present. Like the Egyptian art of death, the effect of the monuments on the modern visitor's sense of time is never made explicit in the novel, but its influence permeates the whole. Charlotte comes to see time as "something liquid, contiguous" (p.67), indeterminate like the many shadows which flit through the book. Nothing, not even death or chronology, is hard and fast in this world, no fixity is ever finally established.

Forster posed muddle and mystery as alternative interpretations of India. Forster's "muddle" is Janice Elliott's "bungle" and there are plenty of examples of this in the book. Mystery is present in the simple sense that, in spite of the successful unearthing of most of the "facts" about Phoebe's death, much remains still unknown at the end; but Janice Elliott's version of Forster's "mystery" goes well beyond an unsolved murder. What is real and what is not real becomes questionable, like everything else, like, particularly, what is life and what is death. Life on the Nile is equivocal, perception itself is unstable. An unseen hand may bring death but equally it can illuminate what was dark: above all, those who venture on this Egyptian passage may cease to be sure what is darkness and what is light, what life is and what death. The title of the novel is seen in hindsight as highly charged, begging at the outset the questions which lie at the heart of it.

> 'Tis life, whereof our nerves are scant,
> Oh life, not death for which we pant;
> More life, and fuller, that we want.

Tennyson's cry of nineteenth century anguish finds its distant echo in ancient Egypt. It is the central paradox of the Egyptian cult of the tomb that it was in fact and in intention a celebration of life. The ankh, a symbol of immortality, lavishly adorns their gods and their figures of the dead and all is provided for an enhanced existence the other side of interment. This paradox continues to exert its fascination in spite of the strongly secular and materialist orientation of twentieth century society. Today's writers, not able or not daring to draw conclusions, offer it for whatever their readers can make of it.

Egypt and the reactions to it of men and women of the nineteenth and twentieth centuries is a topic capable of leading in many directions. The accounts of their Egyptian journeys given by Harriet Martineau, Florence Nightingale and Amelia Edwards have special value because of their individual skills as writers, because of the quality of the minds and temperaments engaged in the writing and because of the relevance of what they had to say to a wide range of interest and enquiry. The three Egyptian books have claims as historical documents with their roots in nineteenth century social and political and religious situations and they connect forwards also to the twentieth century. Each in its own right is a vividly written record of the encounter of a strong mind and personality with a challenging and deeply stirring experience. Those who had once seen Egypt, Harriet Martineau believed, would never feel equally interested in any other country.[15] Florence Nightingale wondered how people could come back from Egypt and live as they had done before.[16] Amelia Edwards gave up one way of life when she returned and adopted another, devoting herself to the rescue and preservation of the Egyptian antiquities. Together they offer a remarkable illumination of personal redefinition under the stimulus of a strong impulse, working on minds already exposed to the competing currents of contemporary life and thought. There is a particular edge to this in that as women, each unmarried, they were exposed to the special tensions endured by independent, active-minded women, seeking a place and a purpose in a society dominated by men. Each triumphed in her way and all three of them, directly or indirectly, injected their experience of Egypt into the bloodstream of their own time and country. What they saw and thought and what they made of it is the subject of the following pages.

Chapter I

Harriet Martineau:
"The Greatest Effort of Courage"

(i)

Harriet Martineau was born in Norwich in 1802, the sixth of eight children of Thomas Martineau, a textile manufacturer and importer of wines, and his wife Elizabeth. The family tradition was Unitarian, a background which was influential in her later thinking. The death of her father in 1826 and consequent financial difficulty led her to decide that she could best provide for herself and her mother by the use of her pen. By the time she died, in 1876, the formidable bulk of her work included novels, histories, publications on social, political and religious questions, travel books and a translation of Comte. She was acquainted with virtually everyone of influence in literary and political circles and could justly write of herself that she had "for a long course of years influenced public affairs to an extent not professed or attempted by many men".[1] Deafness, which began in childhood, increased upon her and for most of her adult life she relied on an ear-trumpet to give her access to social life. She did not allow this disability to inhibit her any more than the fact that she suffered for years at a time from a painful and debilitating illness which confined her to a sickroom. The first onset of this was in 1839 and she spent the next five years in retirement at Tynemouth where she read, wrote and received visits from the many eminent people who journeyed there to see her and, often, consult her. Illness recurred in 1854 and she was convinced, as she had been in the earlier period, that she was dying. It was then that she wrote her autobiography, intending it as the last testimony of a dying woman. In fact, she lived for another twenty years and until 1866 continued to write and, with undiminished energy, to fight for the causes she believed in. The illness, never cured but for years in remission, eventually took hold and became progressively more painful and weakening until the time came when she was forced to give up writing.

She never married though at the age of twenty-four she was briefly engaged to a friend of her brother James. The young man, whose mental and physical health seems never to have been strong, shortly afterwards suffered a total collapse and became incurably insane. She broke off the engagement and mastered with characteristic firmness whatever grief she felt at his death, which occurred a few months later. Reflecting on this episode in her autobiography, she expresses her belief that it was better for her never to have married.[2] Though she acknowledges that there are unsatisfied elements in her nature, contemporary marriage seems to her beset with "evils and disadvantages". It has been the business of her life, she says, to think and to learn, and to speak out with absolute freedom what is in her mind; with that she is content. There is no reason to doubt her word on this. All the evidence of her life and work confirms that matters of the mind always stood high in her estimation and could readily overtop any other consideration. Her two novels, *Deerbrook* and *The Hour and the Man* (to be discussed below) amply bear this out.

She composed her own obituary in 1855, again in the belief that she had not long to live and it is a remarkably cool-headed and perspicacious account that she gives of herself. "She could sympathise in other people's views", she writes, "...and she could obtain and keep a firm grasp of her own, and, moreover, she could make them understood. The function of her life was to do this, and, inasfar as it was done diligently and honestly, her life was of use..."[3] She could have made other claims for herself for she had greater imaginative powers than she allows but what she identifies as her principal gift and function certainly matches the largest part of her career. Her capacity for forming opinions and firmly grasping them, her determination that they should be known and understood and her courage in expressing and maintaining them, in the face of abuse, if need be, and even threat, constitute some of the most admirable parts of her character and contribute to some of her most successful work. These qualities made her a person to be reckoned with but, in the nature of the case, not by any means a universally popular one. Some loved and whole-heartedly praised her. Some began in appreciation and ended in irritation or worse. Some found her a charming, considerate, cheerful companion. Others found their nerves severely tried and there were venom and spite in some attacks. A strongly marked personality will always arouse strong reactions, favourable or otherwise, and Harriet Martineau as a nineteenth century woman claiming for herself a very public role was particularly vulnerable. Like everyone else she had more than one side to her nature and the less attractive sides - a remorseless didacticism and on occasion aggressiveness, for example - were magnified in proportion to her exposure. Tireless herself, she must often have been tiring to others. Hartley Coleridge described her as "monomaniac about everything", a brilliantly witty description of her intensity and single-mindedness which could be applied to one subject after another and even, as he ironically hints, to several subjects simultaneously. There are few areas of Victorian life which she did not take within her scope and on which she failed to leave her mark. She is easy to mock but it is not so easy to emulate her talents and the conscientious and on the whole beneficent use she made of them.

When she went to Egypt at the age of forty-four, she was already an experienced writer. Her father and eldest brother died when she was in her twenties and in 1829 the family business collapsed, making it incumbent on her not only to provide for herself but also to contribute to the family income. She had already become a regular contributor to the *Monthly Repository*, a Unitarian magazine, but under the stimulus of financial need she widened her field. In the 1830s she turned her attention to the newly important and increasingly urgent topic of political economy. Throughout her life her great aim and endeavour was to pass on to others the benefit of the knowledge and understanding which she herself had acquired through thought and experience and her first venture in mass instruction was an unqualified success. She had the idea of couching explanations of economic process and precepts of self-help in the form of short stories to be produced and sold cheaply enough to be within reach of the poor. The narrative form would, she believed, have a popular appeal and the lessons would be swallowed along with the entertainment. The tales that she wrote were an astonishing success, at least in terms of sales and circulation. Nineteenth century readers in all levels of society had a ready stomach for didactic fiction and the "respectable working class" had little enough to feed their imagination on. More richly served readers of a later date can only find the earnest messages too oppressively insistent. Political judgements aside, there is too little vitality in the plots or characterization for these stories now to be anything but documents in a sociologist's casebook but once upon a time they were read avidly. The greater part of her writing in later life was in journalism, travel writing and other forms of non-fiction but the success of her political economy tales encouraged her to publish two full-scale novels in 1839 and 1840. One was a domestic story, *Deerbrook*, and the other, of more ambitious scope and called *The Hour and the Man*, told the story of the Negro hero of Haiti, Toussaint L'Ouverture. The novels, like the stories, are not much read now but they have their merits and are specially useful as an introduction to the mind and imagination which were later to be engaged in her Egyptian book[4]. Fiction, like poetry (which she did not write) may give scope for the freest play of personal qualities and, though all that Harriet Martineau wrote is imbued with character, the novels, both written in her thirties, enable a snapshot to be taken of aspects of her which do not emerge from a brief biographical account.

There is no denying that *Deerbrook* is an excessively solemn novel. The story is of a man (Hope) who falls in love with Margaret, one of two sisters, but the other, Hester, falls in love with him and he is led to believe that it is his duty to marry her. He has a struggle of conscience and comes to accept that he should. Margaret, all innocent of Hope's feelings, goes to live with the married pair. It may look as if the novel is set up for scenes of explosive passion but this is far from being so. The book is heavily religious and the emphasis is all on the duties of selflessness, self-control, renunciation and resignation. There is a vast amount of moralizing dialogue and not the faintest whiff of sexuality. There are suggestions at various points in Harriet Martineau's career that she was squeamish about sex and its absence from this novel is certainly conspicuous. She was later to write about Egyptian harems in a tone very different from that of Kinglake and Warburton and it is perhaps a little amusing that in Enderby, the man with whom Margaret falls in love and who loves her, she creates a figure with instincts very close to those of a harem owner. He allows himself to be deceived by his malicious sister into believing that Margaret knew of and returned Hope's love and that her agreement to marriage with him was intended to cover up the illicit affair. So affronted is he by this alleged failure of purity that he cannot even bring himself to speak a word to Margaret before removing himself from the scene. The thinness and artificiality of motive and character at this and other points show clearly Harriet Martineau's incapacity to deal with sexual relationships. When it comes to the harems, she writes with strong feeling but the topic which rouses her is the less intimate theme of human enslavement and the denial of personal fulfilment.

Virtue is rewarded all round at the end of the novel. Margaret's saintliness is fully established and the wicked sister is punished by the death of her unfortunate daughter. To read *Deerbrook* for the story alone would be madness but the book does not lack interest. There are many more things in it than the nonsense of the plot, notably a strong undercurrent of social concern which involves scenes of suffering among the poor and a demonstration of how ignorance and superstition among them may lead to violence. The middle classes are criticized for their prejudices and the upper class for its irresponsibility. Society's treatment of women also comes in for attention. Maria Young, a governess, is a victim of the denial to women of employment opportunities which might allow them to make use of their talents and energies but this, the novel points out, is only one way in which they suffer social and economic injustice. When, by a convenient death and a will, the Hopes are rescued from penury towards the end of the novel, a point is made of Hope's refusal to accept the whole of the portion made over to himself because he believes that his sisters have not been given a fair share of the family money. That life as presently organized bears hard upon women is a theme which takes its place among the many ideas, about the temper and organization of society and individual responsibility and judgement, which crop up in the novel. Some of them are at least embryonically radical, but in presentation and in the quality of the thinking, the book is immature. The moralizing is glib and the religiosity, earnest and sincere as it is, does not convince that it has been tested by personal enquiry and experience. Harriet Martineau never wavered in her care for the well-being of society and for the right of women to education and full self-development. Nor did she weaken in her adherence to strict moral standards. Her views about religion changed greatly, however, from what they are in *Deerbrook*. The novel emphasizes that the subject was of great importance to her but as time went by her thinking became increasingly adventurous. She is very critical of this earlier work in her autobiography, calling her ideas as expressed there "imperfect and very far from lofty". Her Egyptian journey provoked her to much wider-ranging speculation than anything envisaged in *Deerbrook* and marked the point of no return in her development from the piety of her upbringing and youth to the unorthodox and, in her time, daring position of her later years. Underlying preoccupations remained constant, however, throughout her life: intense concern with moral conduct, its sanctions and its purpose, all inextricably tied in with an understanding of the nature of human destiny, whether that destiny was to be named God, or, as she later thought, science, which, she believed, would come in the fullness of time to be recognized as the ultimately redeeming agent. Egypt brought about the most substantial revision of her views on religion and the nature of humanity and her account of her travels in the east, in effect an intellectual as well as a physical journey, was to provide also the most persuasive form in which to express them.

Deerbrook runs heavily aground on the rock of a story totally unsuitable to the kind of treatment Harriet Martineau was able to give it. The story of Toussaint L'Ouverture is at least a more suitable one for her talents than the somewhat ludicrous concoction of the earlier book. It is not necessarily a more successful novel. It is more homogeneous than *Deerbrook* and the central theme engages Harriet Martineau's attention at a deeper level but the monotoned treatment of character stands out even more sharply. Toussaint L'Ouverture, on whom everything is concentrated, is presented as a figure without stain or blemish of any kind. He suffers stress and anxieties but never deviates in fulfilment of his God-given rôle as redeemer of the Negro race. Ultimately he accepts that this rôle requires that he be sacrificed. He makes the mistake, politically speaking, of trusting the whites too much and is betrayed by them. His tragedy is that the great principle of No Retaliation which he espouses is too elevated for others to follow or even to comprehend. The theme of *The Hour and the Man* is majestic, a passionate rejection of the practice of slavery and of the creed on which it is based. Harriet Martineau will have nothing to do with the argument of innate racial inferiority. She shows blacks capable of all the finer feelings and endowed with moral and intellectual power of a high order. Whatever they lack in actuality is due to deprivation and ill-treatment: in potentiality they are the equals of Europeans and have qualities of open-heartedness and good humour from which Europeans would do well to learn. The stage is a wide one, with a large cast of characters and an extensive range of historical action. The conception is admirable and so, in part, is the execution. It was a considerable feat to amass, interpret and organize the bulk of material which goes into the novel and to set going the range of characters, black, mulatto, and French who are involved. The whole is driven by the author's passionate commitment to the cause but it is that commitment which is responsible also for the lifelessness of L'Ouverture. It is so incumbent upon him to be an example that he fails to be a human being and this failure at the centre is fatal to the novel.

Harriet Martineau's dedication to the anti-slavery cause is one of the noblest aspects of her life and it will be evident again in her account of Egypt. So will, what *The Hour and the Man* also shows, her tolerance of other ways of life and other cultures. She did not by any means subscribe to the out-and-out imperialist view that the white races were the exclusive possessors of wisdom and rectitude and morality. She was open-minded to a degree uncommon in her time and country and to force open a few cracks in the barricaded minds of contemporaries became one of her major endeavours when she encountered the culture of ancient Egypt and was deeply impressed by it. In *Eastern Life* she develops a theory about cumulative enlightenment in religion, each great creed adding some new insight to what has been gained before. There is an earlier version of this in *The Hour and the Man* in the chapter called "Suspense" where Toussaint talks about progressive development in the history of Christianity. According to this, through successive ages the Christian world has come to understand more completely, stage by stage, the nature of Christ's teaching and, gradually, the practice and institutions of nations have been and are being reformed. It is a heavily idealized version of history and one whose terms Harriet Martineau herself would later reject. Though she continued to believe in progressive enlightenment, in her later thinking Christianity itself would appear as only one stage which, like others, had to be surpassed on the way to final illumination.

The Hour and the Man is not without love stories but they do not have anything like the central importance they have in *Deerbrook*. In the later novel it is not sexuality which is prominent by its absence but physicality of another kind. Toussaint L'Ouverture finishes his life in a bare, wet cell which he shares with another man and which he never leaves. Finally he dies alone from thirst and starvation. Realistically imagined this would produce horrifying images of squalor, degradation, disease and torment but no such suggestion is allowed to intrude into the novel. That flesh and blood should be superseded by a disembodied moral conscience is consistent with the generally unrealistic treatment of L'Ouverture and it is also characteristic of Harriet Martineau's enduring belief that mental and moral activity count for more than the merely physical. She had herself a great capacity for carrying on in spite of disability and ill health - Victorians generally, in the absence of modern medicines and techniques, had no option but to be as tough as their constitution and their will would allow them to be and Harriet Martineau's will was amongst the most indomitable. Later, in *Eastern Life*, she would insist that the history of ideas was the real history of man - as opposed to the record of his activities - and the power of ideas is the mainspring of her novel. She goes too far in dematerializing Toussaint L'Ouverture but her misjudgement in this is symptomatic of both strengths and weaknesses. Among her strengths as a novelist are acute powers of observation and she is by no means deficient in imagination. Some areas of experience she cannot deal with but there are also subjects in which she invests the whole weight of her personality and her mind. The driving force of compelling ideas, however, inhibits and obstructs fiction and her gifts are robbed of their full effect by the unsuitable form. In *Eastern Life*, on the other hand, the things which are lacking from her make-up are not forced on the attention and her strong qualities have full play and can be seen at their best: observation, imagination, and the urgent engagement of an ever-active mind with ideas which really constitute for her the essence of human experience. Both *Deerbrook* and *The Hour and the Man* allow a view of some of the most important elements which go to the composition of *Eastern Life* and are there fused into a far richer and more satisfying whole than that achieved in either of the novels or perhaps anything else she wrote. It was her own favourite among her books and there is good reason to agree that she chose rightly.

(ii)

Eastern Life Present and Past is a commodious and tightly packed book. It contains all the basic ingredients of the conventional travel book complete with cast of fellow-travellers, servants and others; it is enlivened by anecdotes; it is lavish of description and energetic in imparting information. It is, however, far from being reducible to any ordinary formula because of the nature of the personality and the quality of the mind which permeate everything. Experience of the Middle East (which nineteenth century travellers commonly called "the East") is a powerful stimulus to Harriet Martineau's imagination and a provocation to intense thought. What results is a compound of personal, social and intellectual elements which gives a unique insight into a remarkable woman and illuminates from an unfamiliar but revealing angle the society which produced her.

The journey described is an extensive one, from Cairo down through Nubia in one direction and to Beirut in another. Travel was by boat, horse, donkey, camel and on foot. On land the route frequently lay over tracks rarely if ever frequented by Europeans. Sometimes tracks of any kind were non-existent. The natives were occasionally unfriendly and precautions had always to be taken against robbers and, in the desert, bedouin. The journey lasted from November 1846 to May 1847. In addition to its travel book-cum-diary quality, *Eastern Life* provides historical background and a detailed account, as full and precise as the author could make it, of the sights to be seen, both man-made and natural. Harriet Martineau had prepared herself by studying the best authorities and she was indefatigable in checking what she could on the spot and also in pursuing her independent investigations. All this area of her work is marked by her dedication to thoroughness and accuracy. Such aspects of *Eastern Life* lie clearly on the surface but there are other layers. Her experience of the tombs and temples of ancient Egypt and the understanding she developed of the religion which they memorialize precipitated a wholesale shift in her mental landscape, rearranging old ideas and introducing new ones. As a result there is a religious/philosophical/metaphysical dimension to *Eastern Life* which adds in no small degree to the fascination of the book. The shape her ideas took, as she thought over what she had seen and learnt in her travels, was such as to outrage her more orthodox contemporaries and to expose her to insult and opprobrium. Though she was not one to flinch when she thought it her duty to speak out, even she had some nervousness at the prospect: "This book", she wrote, "is, I believe, the greatest effort of courage I ever made".[5] In the event the reception, disapproving enough in some quarters, was not as hostile as she anticipated though Murray, the publisher who at first agreed to take it on, later withdrew, fearing that the book would damage his own reputation. It was from Egypt that she received the major impetus for her new thinking and though she travelled extensively beyond its borders it is Egypt which is at the heart of the whole book. In spite of what she saw elsewhere it was the "surpassing interest" of Egypt which claimed her and she counted it as "by far the most interesting portion of our travels".[6] The ancient kingdom is a reference point invoked time and again throughout.

Yet Harriet Martineau's eyes were not focused exclusively on the past. Her acute and active interest in the conditions of her own society led her to observe keenly and enquire pertinaciously into the state of affairs elsewhere. She noted with disapproval the absence of reliable facts and figures in Egypt and took this as itself a sign of inefficient and corrupt government; but on one theme, that of polygamy, she felt she had all the information she needed on which to form strong views. The chapter devoted to harems is a very characteristic one, demonstrating clearly, among other things, how the ideas and responses stimulated by fresh experiences and impressions drew strength and significance from deep roots already planted in her mind and temperament. She was never superficial but everything she saw and learned became a spur to thought and assessment, or reassessment. At the same time, in *Eastern Life* at least, she is rarely ponderous. She shows imagination and sympathy and humanity and even at her most didactic, she commands respect.

Her dauntless persistence in assimilating and relating to each other all the areas of her varied knowledge is admirable though sometimes it produces incongruities of which she herself is serenely unaware. She notes that the women of the harem suffer from indigestion and diagnoses the cause as too sweet a diet and too little exercise; ever practical, she recommends any European doctor who may have access to the sufferers to introduce a skipping rope! Disconcerting in another way is her first response to Petra. She was among the first Europeans to ride through the siq since Burckhardt cut his way through in 1812 and she comments that this "main street", as she calls it, is "badly lighted". This sounds like an extract from a town planner's report, a dismal response to the enchanted entrance to an enchanted city, but Harriet Martineau's resources are not to be lightly dismissed. The fissure in the rocks which makes the entrance to Petra is, she notes, narrow, leaving room for only a strip of sky, "...that 'strip of sky'", her sentence continues, "which one often reads of, but which I never remember to have before seen, except in being drawn up out of a coal-pit"(p.405). It seems safe to assume that not many travellers riding through the siq in Petra have been reminded of being drawn out of a coal-pit. How many ever *have* been drawn out of a coal-pit? The total number is likely to be small: of Victorian ladies in either category it is almost certainly one.

The image of the rose-red city which John William Burgon celebrated in his Newdigate Prize poem[7] may make the nerves tingle but the coal-pit should not be derided. The passage is certainly entirely typical of one side of its author, the woman who made it her business to know about coal-pits and brothels and anything else which touched the life of her time. Whenever possible she looked for herself. Her compulsive desire to take a firm grip on the world around her was far from stopping at purely intellectual matters, predominantly important though she believed they were, and she prided herself on her possession of practical skills. She despised no task which contributed to efficiency or well-being and had no dainty scruples about performing it herself. The crew did the washing on board the dahabieh but it was Harriet Martineau who rose early in the morning to damp and fold the linen. On one occasion she ironed till dinner-time and she firmly reprimands anyone who would laugh at or despise such an activity. An English servant on such a journey, she says, is useless "and the Arabs cannot iron". "If any lady going up the Nile should be so happy as to be able to iron", she concludes, "I should strongly advise her putting a pair of flat-irons among her baggage. If she can also starch, it will add much to her comfort and that of her party" (p.70). There may be a little too much starch here and there about Harriet Martineau, not only in her clothing, but if ever the expression "hands-on" is justified, it fits her exactly. A typical moment occurred during her visit to the Pasha's garden at Shoobra (near Cairo). She found it delightful but "I cannot imagine," she writes, "why the Pasha's windows are so badly glazed." It seemed a golden opportunity for western enterprise to exert itself and for some power to win favour and influence. "Come now!" she exclaims, involving herself in this as in everything else that comes within her view, "which of the politicians of the world will be the first to glaze the Pasha's windows?" Many a one who came in the path of Harriet Martineau's urge for decision and prompt action must have heard her "Come now!" and quailed at it.

This side of her, of course, is not all, nor is her adventurousness. She was willing to defy conventional ideas about what ladies should or should not do and in her travels she allowed nothing to deter her, neither toothache, nor bugs nor scorpions, neither wild dogs nor the claustrophobic atmosphere of barely opened tombs and temples. Her practicality and her intrepidity add to the vitality of *Eastern Life* and to the reader's entertainment but what the book also brings out, and not alone in her descriptions, is an unexpected romantic strain in her nature. Her memory of a coal mine as she rides through the siq is not after all her last word on Petra. During the time she spent there a flash flood occurred. Harriet Martineau was thrilled by the dramatic rush of the waters and went out at night to look at the scene by moonlight. It was not only more spectacular than it had been earlier but it was also startlingly alive. Cliffs and precipices were illuminated by the yellow gleams from fires and wreaths of white smoke rose into the air: "The Arabs had come up from the whole country round, at the sound of the waters; and I had seen Petra populous once more" (p.415). It was, she said, "the most romantic vision of the travels of my life" (p.417).

A poetic sensibility is implicit in her whole response to the torrent in Petra and finds its voice in that last sentence. This is not an isolated instance. The occasion is often, as here, a night scene where her relentlessly acute observing faculty is necessarily dimmed and makes way for other things. "These African nights, soft, lustrous and silent, are worth crossing the world to feel," she writes (p.82) and she made a habit of going out alone after the evening meal to enjoy "the images of the Arab fires, the dim tents and dark camels" and to sing, where no-one could hear her, well-loved songs - an enjoyment, she adds "impossible in our little island where one can never get out of ear-shot!" (p.339-40). In daylight too her strong visual sense can produce pictures that are far from prosaic so that meticulous description is illuminated by an evocative phrase. One view, early in her travels, appeared to her "gay as the rainbow, and as soft as the dawn" (p.35). Often, as in the night scene in Petra, an element of drama sharpens her senses and impresses a picture on her mind. A gale blew up while she was on the Nile and the lives of the whole company were in danger. As she watched the exertions of the crew striving desperately to save the boat from capsizing, even at that moment, she writes, she "could not but be struck" with the picturesque qualities of the scene as the lights from the kitchen and cabin shone on the struggling men and restless sail, slowly and, it seemed, inevitably, descending together to the water (pp.84-85). Her word-pictures, carefully noting the colours and contours of the many views which she exerted herself to seek out, remain enjoyable and evocative. Amelia Edwards, following Harriet Martineau up the Nile some thirty years later, would have the gift to supplement words by the sketches she herself made and a modern visitor takes a camera but Harriet Martineau is at no real disadvantage. Her descriptions not only reproduce what she saw but are also infused with what she thought and felt. When she comments, as she sometimes does, that words fail to convey what the experience of a scene truly was, that some quality in it, though strongly felt, remained inexpressible, the admission of inadequacy itself imparts what Wordsworth called "a certain colouring of the imagination", as no doubt she was aware.

Her eye is sharp and her response to visual stimulus is sensitive but her interest is rarely confined to the eye alone. Mind and imagination alike are engaged when, pondering on the archetypal landscape of Egypt, she writes with striking understanding and sympathy of the significance of "the everlasting conflict of the Nile and the desert" (pp.40-43). From the perpetual need for vigilance against the encroachments of the desert and the annual hope of the seasonal inundation to fertilize the fields, she traces the development of the character and dominant ideas of the ancient society. Ancient Egyptian religious practices, especially the cult of the dead, became more explicable to her as she saw with her own eyes the apparently limitless extent of the western desert, abode of the ever-more-numerous dead, and the thin strip of cultivable land available to the living. That death was greater than life was, she realized, a visible fact imprinted on every consciousness. The journey of the body in its mummy case to its tomb in the rocky cliffs, attended by Anubis the jackal-headed god, would likewise have represented immediate reality to the ancient Egyptians. The Greek story of Charon and the Styx, on the other hand, is to Harriet Martineau's mind merely a vulgarized version of what was in its native place a living myth.

A major element in her approach to her Egyptian experiences is an endeavour to rouse the minds and imaginations of her readers to take in the extraordinary interest and significance of what the archaeologists had uncovered. Egypt's dramatic revelation of "the dark backward and abysm of time" deeply impressed her. Time scales in Egypt extend so far back that imagination falters before that abyss even at the end of the twentieth century, when knowledge of the age of the planet and the countless millennia in which human beings have been active upon it is familiar. Such knowledge was scarcely available and little assimilated when Harriet Martineau wrote. Archbishop Ussher in the seventeenth century had calculated by reference to the Bible that human life had been in existence for a mere six thousand years and it had been assumed that man and the world had been created at the same time. This was a relatively comfortable framework in which to set an individual life but in the early years of the nineteenth century it came under devastating attack from the new science of geology. The hitherto undreamed of dimensions now given to the history of the planet caused great distress to those who realized that other certitudes were also at stake and for whom, as Browning's Bishop Blougram puts it, geology, cosmology and other new sciences rang like little passing bells, each signifying that some faith was about to die. Resistance to the new knowledge was desperate in some quarters but Egypt was a challenge even for those who accepted intellectually the new enlightenment. To entertain the evidence provided by the tombs and temples that a highly developed civilization existed by the Nile three thousand years at least before the Christian era meant a drastic breaking up of understanding and preconception and involved much straining and cracking as the traveller laboriously and painfully tried to adjust his mind-set. To walk into the ancient monuments and see, fresh upon the walls as if the painter or sculptor had just left them, pictures of daily life, and of acts of worship depicted with conviction and immediacy, was to come with shocking intimacy upon lives which had been extinct for thousands of years and yet seemed powerfully present. It was an experience radically to disrupt the perspective in which the life of nations and of individuals was set. To press it upon her readers is a main endeavour of the Egyptian section of Harriet Martineau's book and her rhetorical skills are called upon for maximum effect. At Kom Ombo, for example, she draws attention to the red grid marks by which Egyptians planned their large compositions and points out that these guide-lines were intended to be effaced once they had served their purpose. Two thousand years have passed, however, and they are still there: "No hand, however light, has touched them, through all the intervening generations of men:- no rains have washed them out, during all the changing seasons that have passed over them:- no damp has moulded them: no curiosity has meddled with them. It is as if the artist had lain down for his siesta, with his tools beside his hand, and would be up, presently to resume his work: yet that artist has been a mummy, lying somewhere in the heart of the neighbouring hills, ever since the time when our island was bristling with forests, and its inhabitants were dressed in skins, and dyed their bodies blue with woad to look terrible in battle" (p.160). This is a skilful piece of writing, serving more than one end - not only stirring the imagination but, by its cross-reference from Egyptian time to British, cutting at the heart of insular satisfaction with its own importance and achievement. The upset which Egypt gave to preconceived ideas and assumptions, Harriet Martineau believed, could be nothing but salutary. It taught a becoming humility about the state of contemporary development and - here is the tenderest nerve she touches - it also raised doubts as to whether the most cherished and venerated ideas of the present were really the last and the truest word on such big questions as the relation of man to God and the nature of each.

For it was not only the sense of time and of history which could be enlarged in Egypt. Space once having been created by the displacement of familiar landmarks and their resiting in the vistas of Egyptian time, there was ground for other impressions to take root. She describes the faces of the statues of Rameses II on the exterior of the temple at Abu Simbel as being full of grace but the eight Osirides inside, she writes, "are more. They are full of soul." Egyptian art may depict gods and goddesses as stiff of stance and monotonous of gesture but these figures convey to her eyes a dispassionate benevolence which imparts to them a dignity beyond description. "The difficulty to us now", she adds, "is not to account for their having been once worshipped, but to help worshipping them still" (pp.121-22). These comments on her impressions of Abu Simbel look forward to the point which becomes ultimately the most important of her book: that is, the conclusion to which her travels in Egypt and the other Bible lands led her concerning the origin and history of all religions. As she continued her journey through Syria and Palestine, she studied as she went each of the faiths in turn, the ancient Egyptian, the Hebrew, the Christian and the Mahommedan. The impression made on her by the religion of the ancient Egyptians in its purest form remained with her throughout and much that was best in Christianity and Islam she traced back to that source. Returning to England and preparing her book, she reflected more and more on her sympathy with and admiration for ancient Egyptian thought and the conviction grew in her that no faith truly displaces another. Each in its time answers to the highest aspirations of its adherents and each is to be respected according to the quality of those aspirations. By this criterion she counts the conceptions of ancient Egyptian religion as among the noblest known to history and those who sneer at it and deride it are to her mind both ignorant and unwarrantably complacent. Ultimately, however, her line of thought leads her to the conclusion that all religions have mistaken the true nature and destiny of human existence. Salvation lies not in the supernatural, however envisaged, but in the progress and proper application of science, when humanity will recognize that its rôle is to be its own redeemer and create its own heaven on earth. She accurately forecasts the ever-increasing dominance of science but not - so far - its consequences for humanity. Towards the end of *Eastern Life*, she offers her vision of the new dawn in which science will enthrone "sublime" facts as the true saviours of mankind. There will be "a new order of knowledge and wisdom" when religion - any religion - is finally recognized as a stepping-stone only on the way to realization of full human development. Then the pragmatic intellectual powers of the west will combine with the "Perceptive, Imaginative and Aspiring Faculty of the East" to create "the new heavens and the new earth of the regenerated human mind" (p.565). In this least materialist and most ideal of visions Victorian belief in progress reaches its high water mark.

When, a few years after her return from the Middle East, she attempted to give quasi-philosophic and quasi-scientific form to the latest development of her ideas in a work called *Letters on the Laws of Man's Nature and Development* (published 1850), she made herself an easy prey to the attack and ridicule which *Eastern Life* on the whole avoided.[8] Her readiness to respond to intellectual and imaginative stimulus and her willingness to take risks in following through her responses are features of the earlier book which were, and remain, capable of winning a sympathetic reception. Set out more pretentiously and in more extreme form the flimsiness of the underpinnings of some of her assumptions and conclusions is exposed only too clearly. She was accused of atheism but Florence Nightingale, who remained faithful to Christianity though she defined her own version of it, was nearer the truth when she credited the woman whose mind she knew well with the "truest and deepest religious feeling I have ever known."[9]

When she embarked on her journey, Harriet Martineau had little idea, as she writes in her autobiography, "how the convictions and the action of the remnant of my life would be shaped and determined by what I saw and thought during those all-important months that I spent in the East" (ii, p.277). It is not surprising that the area in which her strongest reactions operated should be religion and that salvation should be envisaged as coming finally through the overwhelming authority of science. Religion had been an urgent preoccupation from her earliest years, Unitarianism and then necessarianism for a time seeming to offer satisfactory answers to questions which pressed upon her. Yet she remained restless and uneasy until Egypt shook her thoughts finally and decisively into a new and abiding pattern. As for the importance of science in her latest thinking, her attitude reflects one of the most energetic and heartfelt concerns of her time. The relation between science and religion was a matter of intense debate and fierce feeling in mid-century England as centuries-old orthodoxies were shaken to the roots. *Eastern Life* provides part of the documentation of that crucial area of Victorian life. Harriet Martineau's emphasis on phrenology and mesmerism was eccentric in her own day and at a later date is even more so but in her prophecy of the decisive rôle of science she identified accurately enough the way the tide was flowing. Her contribution to Victorian life and thought and the interest of her ideas a century and a half later do not derive, however, from her qualifications as a religious thinker, still less do they depend on her authority as a scientist. The greatest value of *Eastern Life* rests in her vigorous and imaginative attempts to prise open closed minds so that they might catch at least a glimpse of wider horizons than conventional English education had prepared them for. Her efforts remain stimulating and can hardly yet be dismissed as superfluous.

She had little patience with those who would go to Egypt merely for a holiday. What is to be found and experienced there is "too suggestive and too confounding to be met but in the spirit of study". "A man who goes to shoot crocodiles and flog Arabs, and eat ostrich eggs, looks upon the monuments as so many strange old stone-heaps, and comes back 'bored to death with the Nile'", she writes with contempt (p.53) but the properly thoughtful traveller, by contrast, can hardly fail to return to his native shore "a wiser, and therefore a better man". To arrive at this desirable state he must not only open his eyes to the lives of the ancient past but his mind also to their ideas and he must be prepared to renounce the timidity and bigotry of those who would suppress new knowledge and deliberately narrow the boundaries of thought.

The extent of her own willingness to enter alien modes of thought, for the sake of whatever enlargement and enrichment they might offer, is strikingly illustrated in the pages she devotes to the practice of mummifying animals (pp.237-42). In lavishly decorated underground chambers dedicated to the gods, she saw countless numbers of mummified cats and birds and well understood the contempt and revulsion felt by the majority of contemporary travellers. She was tempted to share their reactions but reminded herself of one of her most consistent principles: "understand before we despise". Confronted with what she calls "strange positions of the mind", the truly enquiring intelligence will seek without prejudice to find what it was that gave them a hold on the people who believed in them. Nothing, she argues, that has claimed earnest devotion can be dismissed out of hand.[10] The effort to determine cause and motivation will invariably lead to greater understanding of human need and behaviour and so be relevant to conduct and belief in the present time. She sets herself, accordingly, to enquire into what lay behind the Egyptian veneration of animals. She does not pretend to be in a position to treat the subject authoritatively but she offers her speculations as a contribution to sympathetic research. The key element, she suggests, is Egyptian reverence for the sacredness of life and, therefore, of

"Organisation". By organization she means the body, a word evidently too crude to be used without offence just as physical love, that is sex, can, in the same passage, be referred to only obliquely - out of respect, as she says, for "our existing morality and taste". The Egyptians strove to preserve the bodies of their dead, believing them essential to life beyond the grave and, given their respect for the physical constitution of human beings, it was not absurd that they should have extended their care to creatures other than man but similarly endowed with life. Christian revelation promises immortality to man but "not a few Christian philosophers...have shrunk from declaring that beings which enjoy the intellectual and moral powers of the dog, for instance, shall be annihilated at death while Man survives." To the Egyptians, believing that life flowed from an eternal Being and returned to its source on death, no line could be drawn between human beings and animals and reverence was due to the "sentient frame" of all.

The effort to find some common ground between what at first seem two cultures utterly alien to each other does credit to Harriet Martineau's open-mindedness but there is more. She not only wishes to see respectful consideration given to the practices of an ancient civilization but she also wishes to derive lessons for her own society from her reading of the old ideas. She does not deny that the Egyptians may have over-stressed respect for the body but she is at least equally clear that Christians have undervalued it: "The Christian contempt for the body may be found to be an error as great and as mischievous as any heathen worship of it". These are bold words and what follows is bolder: "All that we really know is that we know nothing of absolute creation; that we have no evidence of it, and can form no conception of it: that Life itself is an inexplicable fact to us; that we recognise it only through organisation: and that we have no right, and no power, to conceive of it as apart from organisation". Efforts through the ages to identify an alternative constitution, independent of the body, have failed to produce any evidence while those who attempted it, "in wandering away from the facts of Nature...have injured their own best powers, and failed of the highest attainments possible to their nature". "The supreme presence of facts" is here as ever to be acknowledged before all else. We know we have bodies: we know

38

little else. The legitimate conclusion, according to Harriet Martineau, is not that we should subordinate the body to some ascetic ideal but that we should cultivate it. The fully developed human being will be one in whom a splendid physique provides the conditions for a perfectly functioning brain and together they produce "the highest moral and intellectual elevation possible to humanity".

This vision of a super-race of the future goes as far beyond the "facts" as any of the other visions which she dismisses as fantasies but her plea for the dignity of the body in an age of draped piano legs was brave and forward-looking. When she is less caught up with proselytizing for the empire of fact, she puts her point in less extreme ways, deploring, for example, the restraints put by English parents on the natural freedom and spontaneity of children's movements and noting with approval, when she is in America, how much more encouragement is given there to healthy exercise for young people. The mummy pit pages would be less engaging reading than they are, however, if the arguments were presented with more qualification and caution. Harriet Martineau is here in the full flow of various enthusiasms (phrenology, appropriately enough her King Charles's head, makes an appearance) and the passage is alive and warm with them. The pelting with ideas from a multitude of directions is exhilarating even if, on examination, some of them tend to melt away in the hand. Eventually the excitement subsides and the chapter is brought to a calm and weighty close. There are many disappointments, Harriet Martineau writes, in exploring "the only true history of Man - the history of Ideas" (p.241), for every faith by which mankind has so far been guided has sooner or later gone astray and lost itself in "a dim world of dreams", but the "great governing Ideas of mankind" have never been extinguished. Her list of these, "Moral Obligation and strict retribution, the supreme desirableness of moral good, and the eternal 'beauty of holiness'", reflects her time and country. She was prepared to voyage on strange seas of thought, alone if need be, but she could always find anchor in the secure bed of moral rectitude and noble aspiration, laid down by her Unitarian upbringing and reinforced by the temper of her class and her society.

She had no doubt that refusal to open the mind to what other societies can teach was a regrettable limitation of human potential. Development, she was confident, will only come through the clear-sighted and fearless pursuit of knowledge and whatever impedes this must be an evil. At a later stage of her travels, in Palestine, she was moved by what she called the "superstitious" practices of many Christians to inveigh with special indignation against the bibliolators - those who insisted on the literal truth of the Bible and refused to make any critical assessment of evidence. Bibliolatry is worse, she declares, than idolatry for idolatry, Christian or pagan, involves at least some true idea whereas bibliolatry is a perversion, distorting the spirit for the sake of extolling the letter. She goes on to make a formidable indictment of its effects on the intellectual world at home: "our faithless and irreverent timidity has so grown upon us...that it would be an act of great courage in divines of our day to publish what divines a century ago were honoured for publishing" (p.441). Scientists, philosophers and historians, she claims, are deterred from publishing what they find to be true or exposing what they know to be false. Such passages underline again that *Eastern Life* is more than a travel book and more also than a personal record, however interesting in both these respects it is. It is also a document of Victorian life and thought and Harriet Martineau fully intended that the thoughts to which her Eastern experiences led her should be infused with as much force as she could muster into the consciousness of her own society.

(iii)

The full title of her book recalls Thomas Carlyle's *Past and Present* of 1843 but the inversion, no doubt deliberate, distinguishes it. The contents and purposes of the two books are in any event very different. In Carlyle's hands the contrast between then and now works persistently to the shame of the present and, though Harriet Martineau also belabours her society from time to time, it is the state of English intellectual life with which *Eastern Life* is on those occasions concerned, not its social and industrial systems. The state of society and the condition of the peasants in contemporary Egypt do, however, concern her. Harriet Martineau had a genuine feeling for the people. Far from sharing the contempt affected by many of her countrymen, she liked the Arabs she encountered, the dragoman, for instance, who served her party during the whole of their journey. His qualities were not exceptional among his people, she believed, and, thinking of the Europeans who employed him and men like him, she adds: "I felt that some of us might look very small in our vocations, in comparison with our dragomen" (p.13). Towards the crew in general her attitude was affectionate and motherly. To behave with coldness and severity was not the way to treat them, she insisted, and she is at pains to record that, in the experience of English travellers she met on her journey, there were no stories of robbery or violent behaviour on the part of the Arabs. She did herself, in fact, have two unpleasant experiences when wandering off on her own but she blames herself for putting temptation in the way of "poor creatures" who could not resist the opportunity to extract money if they could (p.175). Sympathetic understanding is in evidence in all her experiences with ordinary people. When a small child is whisked up on board by one of the sailors, she is fascinated by his terror and wonders what it is that he so much fears. A gift of some raisins makes him happy but he is still off like a shot as soon as he is released. Putting herself in his place she imagines that his adventures on the strange foreign boat will be a family anecdote for generations to come (p.137). Her large mindedness even extends to tolerance when she is insulted as an immodestly clad infidel in Cairo: "I really did not wonder at it; and could not resent it, putting myself in the place, for the moment, of a devout Mohammedan" (p.287).

However much she liked the crew and sympathized with the poor, there was no getting away from the overall degeneration of Egypt. As her party takes its last view of Karnak, she reflects that here, on the plain of Thebes, the human intellect had been enthroned while humanity elsewhere remained primitive. "And how was it now?" she asks. "That morning I had seen the Governor of Thebes, crouching on his haunches on the filthy shore among the dung heaps, feeding himself with his fingers, among a circle of apish creatures like himself" (p.217). She was alert, as always, to the sights and sounds and people of the present and responsive to the pictorial qualities of her environment but, again as always, she was too thoughtful to yield herself completely to the spell of the picturesque. Cairo was a delight: "there is nothing so wonderful and romantic in the whole social world as an Arabian city; and Cairo is the queen of Arabian cities" (p.275). To enjoy it, however, uncomfortable reflections must be suppressed. Not only must ancient Egypt be forgotten with all it stood for but the visitor must also "shake off any considerate humanity which may hang about him". The shows of things are enchanting, provided one does not look at what lies underneath. As with the social life of the streets, so with the appearance of the people. Their physical condition appears to compare well with that of the poor in England but they are afflicted by deep-seated ills of another kind. In a chapter devoted specifically to the present condition of the country, Harriet Martineau offers her findings with some diffidence, aware that as a passing visitor she is not qualified to speak with authority. Nevertheless she has tried hard to inform herself and the fact, which she soon encounters, that accurate information is impossible to come by is taken as prime evidence of gross mismanagement and misdirection on the part of the government. Any attempt to enquire about population trends, rates of payment or extent of taxes runs up each time against endemic corruption, bribes, illegal exactions and administrative folly or worse. Muhammad Ali, for all his attempts to improve the country, has omitted to guarantee to his people property and other rights which she believes indispensable to real progress. Ostentatious public works may be put in hand but "no such spectacle is ever seen as a native bettering his condition, or attempting to do so" (p.309). The chapter is a brief one for Harriet Martineau is scrupulous in including nothing which she has not, at least in some degree, been able to check for herself. Firsthand knowledge was always to her a priority and she spared no pains to acquire it, whether in a coal-mine or, as it appears, in a brothel.

She visited two harems while she was in the Middle East, one in Cairo and one in Damascus, and whatever hesitations she felt about pronouncing on the national government, she had none about expressing her view of this feature of domestic life. She approached the subject of polygamy according to her usual principle, that alien ideas and practices should not be condemned out of hand but should be studied open-mindedly, with the assumption that anything which has gained wide and long acceptance must have at least something to be said for it. In this instance, closer acquaintance leads not to greater sympathy but to increased revulsion. Willingness to study and understand the faith of ancient Egypt had opened up new and, she believed, richly enhancing vistas in her mind. What she saw and learned in the harems worked differently for it served not to modify or extend but to reinforce other ideas which she had held long and passionately. The harem chapter, consequently, is not exploratory but is instead infused with the concentrated energy of convictions strongly held.

The subject was a difficult one for her to handle, given her own fastidiousness and the restrictions of her society. She was never one to shirk speaking out when her conscience dictated it but she shrank on this occasion from reporting all she saw and knew, believing, or persuading herself, that any good which might be done by greater explicitness would not balance the shock and distress caused to her readers. To be inhibited from approaching the subject of sex directly might seem to be a crippling limitation on any serious account of a harem but self-censorship in this instance is less damaging than might be supposed. The essence of polygamy, as Harriet Martineau sees it, is the denial to fellow human beings of the right to personal dignity and self-fulfilment. This is where the emphasis lies in the one oblique reference to the sexual services rendered by the women of the harem. She found, she says, "no traces of mind" in any of the inhabitants, except one old woman (p.297). All the young ones were "dull, soulless, brutish or peevish" and, she goes on: "How should it be otherwise, when the only idea of their whole lives is that which, with all our interests and engagements, we consider too prominent with us?" In her diary that night she noted: "here humanity is wholly and hopelessly baulked". For one to whom humanity was sacred, there could be no worse crime than that. She considers with intense pain the new life which is born in the harems - if the child is a girl, she "sees before her from the beginning the nothingness of external life, and the chaos of internal existence". If a boy, living among the women and the eunuchs for his first ten years, he sees and learns things which brutalize him for life. It is her understanding that not many children are, in fact, born in large harems as indeed not many are born in brothels (identified as "the houses at home which morally most resemble these harems" (p.294)). In harems and in brothels the rare new lives are likely to be idolized and finally pampered to the extent that even if born healthy they die of excessive indulgence; or, in the harem, they may be murdered by another woman jealous of the mother and Harriet Martineau has a nightmare vision of "the mother and the murderess, always rivals and now fiends, being shut up together for life" (p.295).[11]

Concubines and eunuchs for the harems were largely provided by the importing of slaves, both black and white, the supply being organized by Christian traders, a fact bitterly noted by Harriet Martineau. Slavery and polygamy, "two hellish practices" (p.299), were always, she believed, intimately connected and in Egypt they were clearly seen to be inseparable. This was not her first encounter with slavery for she had spent two years in America, 1834-36, travelling extensively in the north and the south. Though firmly convinced that slavery was indefensible on any count, she refrained as long as she could from open statement of her views so as not to be restricted in the people she could meet and the places she could visit; but when called upon at an abolitionist meeting to express support, she had no alternative. She braved insult and even physical danger in her championship of the slaves and what she saw and heard made her even more committed to the cause of abolition. When she returned home she worked for it by every means in her power. She also worked with similar whole-hearted vigour for the cause of women, a campaign also given extra stimulus by her American experience[12]. Oppression by the strong, whether of women or of slaves, had always to be resisted. Slavery and polygamy, whether in Egypt or Carolina, were to her mind but two faces of the same thing.

The linking of polygamy and slavery is the keynote struck throughout the chapter on harems. As is her wont, Harriet Martineau reports fully and with care for accuracy on what she observes of dress and manners and incidents but here less than anywhere, even if she were ever tempted to it, was she likely to be content with superficial observation. The harems are far from being merely picturesque to her, exotic material for a traveller's

44

notebook, but they touch at the heart of human claims to dignity and the human obligation of respect one to the other. The contrast between her account and the light-hearted (not to say frivolous) observations of some of her male contemporaries does not need to be laboured. Even from the harem in Damascus, where the visit was pleasanter than in Cairo, she leaves with a sense "of the most injured human beings I have ever seen" (p.304). *Eastern Life* proclaims throughout that ideas constitute the real history of man and the ideas underlying slavery and polygamy being, as she believed, evil beyond amendment, it followed that rottenness pervaded all Egyptian life. No words could be too strong for the extent and depth of the viciousness engendered: "if we are to look for a hell upon earth, it is where polygamy exists: and...as polygamy runs riot in Egypt, Egypt is the lowest depth of this hell" (p.293). Not everything in modern Egypt seemed to her to be hellish but the abuse of human dignity represented by polygamy cast a deep shadow over all the rest.

Eastern Life Present and Past is a valuable book, valuable because of its connections with wide areas of Victorian life and thought, valuable for its vivid account of travel in Egypt in the early years of its opening up to foreign tourists and valuable for the opportunity it gives to become well acquainted with the mind and imagination and personality of a woman who is at the same time formidable and vulnerable, forbidding but warm-hearted. She is no more without her faults than any other acquaintance but she is very seldom boring and she is always capable of surprising with a phrase, a thought or an unexpected dip into her vast reservoir of things done, places visited, experiences gained. She is a practised writer and she knows how to use rhetorical build-up for striking effect but there is no deceit or insincerity in her skills. Egypt made a dramatic impact on her and it resulted in a multi-layered and fascinating book, illuminating and entertaining on many levels, a work which is a credit both to her and, in spite of her criticisms of her own society, to the age which produced her.

Chapter II

Florence Nightingale:
"God spoke to me at Karnak"

(i)

Of the three women at the centre of this book Florence Nightingale is today by far the best known but her *Letters from Egypt*[1] belong to the part of her life before she came into public view and entered folk-memory as "the lady with the lamp". She was twenty-nine when she went to Egypt. The date was 1849 and it would be another four years before the Crimean War broke out and gave her freedom to do the work she felt she was born for. The letters themselves, addressed to her family, are lively, informal, often amusing. Unlike Harriet Martineau, she was writing for a private audience and she had no educational or other programme in mind. She does describe the sights she sees and she does record her thoughts but it is one of the attractions of what she writes that her responses are spontaneous and not subject to after-thought and reorganization. The situation is not quite so transparent as it may seem, however. Florence Nightingale did not record *all* she thought and felt in her letters. She kept at the same time a diary and the story told there makes it only too plain that the woman who wrote home so entertainingly was at the time suffering intense mental torment. The letters are, in fact, multi-dimensional, as *Eastern Life* is, but differently so. They give a traveller's account of the sites of the Nile and they at the same time draw from and contribute to the world of Victorian life and thought. Like Harriet Martineau's, they gain their special interest from the strong impress of a particular personality but, unlike *Eastern Life*, Florence Nightingale's letters also offer a unique and dramatic insight into an inner life which she could confide to few of her contemporaries. Little attention has been paid to her Egyptian visit but the letters, illuminated by the diary, constitute a record which is a crucial document in the history of her life. To set them in their context is, in the circumstances, particularly needful.

46

Florence Nightingale was born in 1820, the second daughter of well-to-do parents. They divided their time between London and a house in the country and moved among the "best" society in both locations. It was natural for Mrs Nightingale to look forward to social success for her daughters, an object most likely to be attained through marriage. Young Florence was attractive and there was no shortage of eligible suitors but the advantages of the life so readily available failed to impress her. When Richard Monckton Milnes proposed she was indeed tempted but felt, almost in spite of herself, that marriage was not the way of life for her. Her attitude and her aspirations were quite beyond the comprehension or the sympathy of her parents and her sister. As early as 1837 she believed that God had specifically called her and required of her some service. What its nature was she did not then know but gradually over the following years, as she seized what opportunities she could to break away from the stultifying routines of home, care of the sick seemed ever more certainly to be the rôle she was meant for. To be sure of this was far from being able to achieve it. Nursing at that date was among the lowest occupations in public esteem and reasonably so, for the women who undertook it were commonly drunken and degraded. Dickens's Sarey Gamp is unrealistic only in being amusing and amusing only to those who are safe from her ministrations. Hospitals were insanitary and incompetent and the benighted state of the medical profession in general is well attested. It seemed madness for any well brought-up young lady to contemplate immersing herself in such a scene. Nevertheless Florence Nightingale persevered and prepared herself by extensive study against the day when her chance would come. Once or twice she thought she had won her parents over but time and again she was frustrated and the bitterest despair would overwhelm her as it seemed that release was as far away as ever from a family bondage which threatened to kill her or drive her mad.

She early formed the habit, retained till she was old, of writing down the thoughts and feelings which no one in her circle could sympathize with or understand. Many of these private notes have survived. It is in one of them that she recorded that "On February 7th, 1837, God spoke to me and called me to his service".[2] The

47

very next day the Nightingales sailed for France on their way to Italy and the seventeen year old Florence, far from weighed down by a sense of divine calling, plunged into an orgy of dancing and partying. Her intellectual and moral world was expanding, however, and by the time the family returned to England in the spring of 1839 she was ready, eager indeed, to hear again the call to God's service. It was to be another fourteen years before she could enter upon what was to be her life's work and in the meantime she remained bound to a treadmill of social engagements and family duties which became agony to her. Her visit to Egypt came towards the end of the long and anguished period of waiting to fulfil what she was convinced was her mission in life; but she did not know that the door which had been so inexorably shut was about to open and the months in Egypt were a time of mental agony.

The evidence is in the diary she kept but the background against which the diary and the Egyptian letters are to be seen is painted elsewhere, in "Cassandra", part of the second volume of a longer work which Florence Nightingale wrote in 1852. The book was never published but "Cassandra", extracted from it, appeared in 1928 as an appendix to Ray Strachey's history of the Women's Movement in Great Britain.[3] It is not a polished composition; it is repetitive and written as if the pen itself were almost choked with anger as it inscribed the words on the page; but it is nevertheless extremely valuable. In effect it is the story of Florence Nightingale's years of frustration as she was pinned down by the prohibitions and expectations imposed on women of her station and by the loyalty and affection for her family which prevented her from cutting herself loose from them. "Why have women passion, intellect, moral activity - these three - and a place in society where no one of the three can be exercised?" she demands (Strachey, p.396). What society does ask of women, she goes on, is to fritter away their time and their intelligence in trivial occupations and meaningless social rounds. Required always to be at the call of someone else, for no matter how petty a reason, they can never seriously study nor achieve. The domestic duties which are urged on women as sacred are really nothing but bad habits, handed down from mother to daughter. The family itself, for which supreme importance is claimed, is, in fact, "too narrow a field for the development of an immortal spirit, be that spirit male or female. The chances are a thousand to one that, in that small sphere," (and here unmistakably is the dread that haunted Florence Nightingale's life) "the task for which that immortal spirit is destined by the qualities and gifts which its Creator has placed within it, will not be found" (Strachey, p.404). Young women, shut up in themselves and tormented by energies for which they have no outlet, dream of an ideal companion to whom they may talk freely and with whom they can share lives full of the interest and meaning which are lacking in their own. Such dreams are natural but society's wilful blindness to the needs of youth makes it appear that they are shameful." "We fast mentally, scourge ourselves morally, use the intellectual hair-shirt, in order to subdue that perpetual day-dreaming, which is so dangerous! We resolve 'this day month I will be free from it'; twice a day with prayer and written record of the times we have indulged in it, we endeavour to combat it. Never with the slightest success...It is the want of interest in our life which produces it" (Strachey, p.397). All this is painful to read, all the more painful for its revelation of what was an intimately personal experience. In 1852 "Cassandra" claims that "dreaming" is natural and, if blameable at all, to be laid to the account of hostile circumstances; but the diaries, not only during the Egyptian visit but much later in her life, show that "dreaming" persisted. Wish-fulfilment fantasies, born originally of her frustrated youth, became part of an enduring psychological pattern. Taught to believe that they were disgraceful, she continued throughout her life, whatever form they took, to regard them with deep shame and guilt.

"Cassandra" counts among the evils of a young lady's life the time wasted in writing innumerable letters, mere social gestures with no point or purpose in themselves. The time spent did at any rate give her facility with her pen so that when she really had something to communicate she could do it with bite and energy. "Cassandra" is too headlong and disorganized to be as a whole well-written but individual passages drive their point home with a vigour which derives very largely from the use of telling imagery and example. She gives, for instance, a memorable description of the experience of being read aloud to. Most social gatherings, she says, are vacuous and deliberately so but sometimes, as a "literary exercise", everyone reads aloud out of a book or newspaper. This is both insult and agony. "What is it to be 'read aloud to'?...It is like lying on one's back, with one's hands tied and having liquid poured down one's throat. Worse than that, because suffocation would immediately ensue and put a stop to this operation. But no suffocation would stop the other" (Strachey, p.402). The violence of this image of enforced passivity and the fierce resentment it conveys at suppression of individual choice and judgement carry the force of her rage and show the power of self-expression she has at her command. Other tactics are equally dramatic: "If we have no food for the body, how do we cry out, how all the world hears of it, how all the newspapers talk of it, with a paragraph headed in great capital letters, DEATH FROM STARVATION! But suppose one were to put a paragraph in the *Times*, Death of Thought from Starvation, or Death of Moral Activity from Starvation, how people would stare, how they would laugh and wonder! One would think we had no heads nor hearts by the total indifference of the public towards them. Our bodies are the only things of any consequence" (Strachey, pp.407-8). "The next Christ", she says boldly, "will perhaps be a female Christ", but she does not pursue that idea.

"Cassandra" is a protest on behalf of all women and it is also a personal cry from the heart of one particular woman, uttered from the depths of experiences which were, to her in particular, literally intolerable. Much of what she says has the wider social relevance she assumes but it is also true that hers was a singular nature, powerful, complex and difficult. Certainly she baffled her family, who could never cope with her. What she writes about women and society is not only a social document, angrily cataloguing the many evils stemming from the suppression of women; it is also an explosive discharge of thought and feeling of an exceptional individual, writing out of an exceptionally pressurized situation. This individual in this situation and this state of mind went to Egypt in 1849 and left a double testimony to her experiences, in her letters and in her private diary. The letters themselves need to be read with a kind of double vision, attending to what there is on the surface and also to the rocks and under-currents which lie beneath and to which the diary, and "Cassandra" also, clearly point.

(ii)

The *Letters from Egypt* have a different tone from "Cassandra", as they obviously must, given the different subject-matter and different expected audience. Humour is not constantly submerged in irony and the field of observation is necessarily much wider. Yet the same vigorous and sharply edged mind is at work. The acerbic quality which marks "Cassandra" is by no means absent and social life and expectation, not quite escapable even on the Nile, are dismissed, if not so mordantly at least with contempt only slightly veiled.[4] The telling use of concrete imagery which does so much to vivify "Cassandra" enlivens the *Letters* also and there are the first shoots of broad speculation about religious and social matters which are to burgeon a few years later in the work, *Suggestions for Thought*, of which "Cassandra" forms part.[5] Some of the emotional pressures which shape these are discernible when, after a month spent in Alexandria and Cairo, she had her first experience of the desert. The impression which it makes, she writes, "is ever new, ever inconceivable...It is not the absence of life, but the death of life which makes it so terrible...the idea perpetually recurring of an awful devil at work, making this kingdom his own, overwhelming everything by some monstrous convulsion". The earth is "hope-less and helpless" and, contemplating it, "one almost fancies one hears the Devil laughing as he dares even Almighty power to bring forth bread" (p.49). Harriet Martineau had also found the desert inconceivable. Before she experienced it she thought she was able to imagine what it was like: having taken her first ride in it, she believed that nobody could. In its lack of feature, its suffocation and glare, it is, she writes, "the very home of despair";[6] but Harriet Martineau herself did not despair. She thought of death but she also noted life - dragonflies flitting about where there seemed to be no possibility of water and beetles going about their business and leaving their tracks in the sand. Her eye was as keen here as everywhere: "Distant figures are striking in the Desert, in the extreme clearness of light and shade...It seems to me that I remember every figure I ever saw in the Desert...Every moving thing has a new value to the eye in such a region".[7] The passage is typical of her. She recognizes the invitation to despair but in her energy of mind and zest for activity she throws it off.

Florence Nightingale's reactions are in strong contrast. She took no note of dragonflies or beetles. Still less did she find any glamour in distant figures in the landscape. Her response to what she saw is powerful but above all deeply disturbed and disturbing. In the lifeless, "frightful" desert she discerned the hand of the devil at work and acknowledged his potency. The physical features of Egypt led Harriet Martineau to ruminate on how "the everlasting conflict" of Nile and desert had fed "the ideas, the feelings, the worship, the occupation, the habits, and the arts of the people of the Nile valley, for many thousand years",[8] but Florence Nightingale interpreted it differently. For her it was the contrast between the earth and the sky which was significant and what it signified was a struggle between God and the devil. The desert was dead and without beauty; the sky on the other hand was radiant, light pouring from every part of the brilliant sky: "the earth seems the abode of the Devil, the heavens of God" (p.49). The devil had a reality which impinged strongly on Florence Nightingale at this time. What she saw as a struggle between him and God was waging in her mind throughout the Nile journey and neither the company of friends nor the observation of customary codes of behaviour could save her from his presence. God had called her in 1837 but twelve years later she was as far from entering on her mission as ever. It must be, she told herself, because she had sinned and was unworthy and she tormented herself day after day wrestling in the greatest anguish with herself and with her Lord.

The difference between the secret text which underlies the letters she sent home and the story told by the letters themselves is dramatic. In her diary she constantly accuses herself of the dreaming which she writes of so painfully in "Cassandra", that lapsing from the world around to lose herself in imagination of other circumstances and other company. She dreams, she writes with disgust, even "in the very face of God". Coming down-river in February 1850, she notes after a day's sightseeing: "Where was

Harriet Martineau in domestic mood. (Pl. 1)

Florence Nightingale, from a carte de visite. (Pl. 2)

Amelia Edwards. (Pl. 3)

Lucie Duff Gordon. (Pl. 4)

A Street in Cairo. "There is nothing so wonderful and romantic in the whole social world as an Arabian city; and Cairo is the queen of Arabian cities": Harriet Martineau. (Pl. 5)

Kom Ombo, a double temple dedicated to Horus and Sobek, the Hawk and the Crocodile. Amelia Edwards calls the ruins "a magnificent torso". (Pl. 6)

Village scene. (Pl. 7)

Obelisk and great hypostyle hall, Karnak. Of this "immeasurable forest of col-
umns" Florence Nightingale wrote: "They are like him to whom they are
dedicated, 'ineffable'". (Pl. 8)

The Colossi of Memnon. The inundation is retreating and the mud is cracking.
Medinet Habu is seen in the distance on the right. (Pl. 9)

Philae, Kiosk of Trajan. Amelia Edwards refers to it by another name, "Pharaoh's Bed". (Pl. 10)

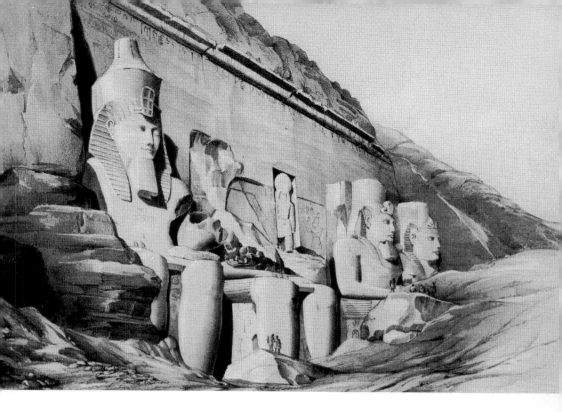

Exterior of the Great Temple, Abu Simbel, showing the colossal figures of Ramesses II. Florence Nightingale found them "sublime in the highest style of intellectual beauty". (Pl. 11)

Amelia Edwards's sketch of part of Luxor Temple showing on the roof the so-called French House where Lucie Duff Gordon lived. Amelia Edwards wrote that the view made the poverty of the place splendid. (Pl. 12)

I all the while...dreaming." On the voyage up-river she had visited and been deeply impressed by the ruins of Karnak but now, she feels despairingly, "Karnak itself cannot save me now. It has no voice for me". She was wrong, however, for Karnak did speak - or more precisely, the little temple of Goorneh also at Thebes. The rare luxury of a morning to herself allowed her to sit for hours on the steps of the portico and there, "God spoke to me again". This was the opening of weeks of intense private experience, all the more intense for being crowded into the brief periods she had to herself, but no hint of this appears in the letters she sent home. The morning at Goorneh is described there and the "matchless view" but the only voices recorded are those of birds, "the first I have heard in Egypt" (pp.143-44).

Florence Nightingale's torment of mind was to recur all her life. Free for half an hour in her cabin on March 9th, 1850, she wrote that she had "settled the question with God" and on the 15th, rejoiced that "God has delivered me from the great offence and the constant murderer of my thoughts"; but this was a temporary respite only. The struggle was to submit herself to the long ordeal of waiting for her destiny to be fulfilled and to be prepared to resign herself even if, after all, it never should be fulfilled. The terror was the "dreaming" which she could not control and which she believed was an offence to God and disqualified her from achieving anything. It seemed like incipient madness. It seemed even more terribly to be satanic possession. She was "sold", she writes "to the enemy", "My enemy is too strong for me...all, all is in vain", and she spent days of "absolute slavery" in his thrall.

It is terrible to turn from the outpourings of 1850 to a small diary of 1877 and find the flyleaves covered with painful expressions of the same anguish wracking her still. The circumstances are different and she has years of extraordinary achievement behind her but she is no less agonized by the thought that she has sinned and, through sin, has failed, and all her efforts have been rendered vain. Underlying the later crisis and throwing light on those of earlier years is her fear that she is driven by lust for reputation and that this undermines what should be service only to God. According to one note, a dialogue took place at seven o'clock in the morning on December 7th, 1877. The voice of God asked her: "If I do what you want about the Indian irrigation, would you give up all your name in it?" and she answers, "Yes, Lord, I think I would", and then: "Yes, Lord, I am sure I would".[9] It seems clear that the intense frustration she felt as a young woman, when baulked of her burning wish to be allowed to nurse, left an indelible mark. She suffered intolerable stress when she met, as she often did, obstruction and frustration in carrying out the schemes which seemed to her to be self-evidently and urgently needed. Early in her life and later, the frustration was associated in her mind with the idea of some guilt of her own, specifically in later years with vainglory, the wish to be acclaimed for what she did. No doubt that is why she rejected all plans to honour her for her work in the Crimea and why she declined the offer of a national funeral and burial in Westminster Abbey. Whether fame and reputation made part of the "dreams" that so fascinated and appalled her in Egypt is not knowable nor indeed can it be certain that the fear of acting for self-glorification was ever anything other than an attempt to accommodate severe frustration by a kind of rationalization. To assign an internal cause to account for an external effect may offer some possibility of controlling, or at least influencing, a situation which is otherwise totally intolerable.

The diary and "Cassandra" compose a sub-text the marks of whose influence on the letters are clearly visible. The insistent presence of the devil is noticeable, for example, when Florence Nightingale hears "the most supernatural noise" in the temple at Dendera, and at once likens it to "the sighing of devils in hell" (p.159). She comments more than once on her sense of living among people "who know not what they are put in the world for" (p.71), the very question which most oppresses herself. With some cynicism and evidently with reference to the same point, she writes, à propos the title "Lord of Justice", assigned to a pharaoh, that it was "a mistake as old as the world and as young as our time, to suppose oneself called to a power one has not, to do a thing which is not one's business" (p.145). The state of modern Egypt and Egyptians she sees as one of "deep, grinding, brutalising misery" (p.176) yet God's promise of salvation is to all "and therefore Egypt *will* be saved and therefore one can believe, even of *these* creatures, that 'it is good for them to be here' - I believe in God, and therefore Egypt is not hell, as one would otherwise believe" (p.193). Preoccupations of her own mind are apparent in all this, the ever-imminent presence of "the enemy", the sense of uselessness, the striving for resignation - if necessary to inactivity - and the hope that God will indeed save, and that neither Egypt nor her own life will for ever be hell.

The tempestuous state of her mind is reflected also in the oscillations in her attitude to what she sees in her travels. At times she is ostentatiously philistine. She could not "muster a single sensation" at her first sight of the pyramids (p.31) and became only more scathing on closer acquaintance. There was nothing to be said about the colossi at Thebes other than that they were big and ugly. She is being deliberately "shocking" in her dismissal of these high points of cultural tourism but even when other qualities impress her she continues to find ugliness characteristic of Egypt: "There is nothing beautiful in Egypt" (p.72) and even "everything in Philae is *ugly*" (p.114). A recent visit to Italy had filled her with delight in the splendours of Italian art and in Egypt she persisted in referring back to its masterpieces. Harriet Martineau was willing to consider alien forms on their own terms[10] but Florence Nightingale in her chafed and inflamed state of mind was less prepared for the exercise of broadening her sympathies in this way.

The differences in tone and character between the two accounts of Egypt are many and obvious. A measure of common ground develops, all the same, between the Martineau and the Nightingale responses as, almost against her will, Florence Nightingale found herself stirred by the monuments and what she took to be their meaning. At Beni Hassan she cared little to know whether a painting did or did not represent Joseph and his brethren: "All that one wants to know is, that on this soil nearly 4000 or 5000 years ago men stood who felt and thought like us, who cared for their brothers, and mourned over their dead with an everlasting love and preserving memory like us - that memorials of their love have remained while all remembrance of them has passed away..." (p.54). This is, at least in part, a reaction against European insistence on seeing everything in terms of their own culture instead of opening their minds to what was to be learnt of another. She is similarly irritated later when, at Karnak, visitors behave as though a representation of Rehoboam on the walls was the only thing worth looking at: "Oh, I was so sick of it" - all the more so because "we don't know anything which makes Rehoboam so very interesting to us" (p.140). As she saw and learned more of the tombs and temples, her feelings about them deepened and at Ipsamboul (Abu Simbel) her enthusiasm was intense. She writes of the four colossal figures on the façade of the great temple: "Sublime in the highest style of intellectual beauty; intellect without effort, without suffering...the whole effect is more expressive of spiritual grandeur than anything I could have imagined" (p.97). She is much moved by the Osiris figures in the interior: "'Full of grace and truth', as his inscription bears, indeed he looks." She accepts Osiris as "the incarnation of the goodness of the deity...and I thought how beautiful the idea which placed him in the foremost hall, and then led the worshipper gradually on to the more awful attributes" (p.98).

At the beginning of the journey she had very much enjoyed the beauty that she found in the streets of Cairo but was in a mood to be unimpressed by the regulation sights of ancient Egypt. Abu Simbel, however, finally won her over as the atmosphere of the ancient places penetrated her imagination and reassembled the furnishings of her mind. "Egypt is beginning to speak a language to me, even in the ugliest symbols of her gods", she writes (p.104), and the metaphor she uses is a significant one. As she grew familiar with the Egyptian gods and the way in which they were represented in the monuments, the ideas of ancient Egypt began to mesh in with her own religious preoccupations. One relief at Abu Simbel particularly struck her. As she describes it, it shows "the great Rameses crowned by the good and evil principle on either side" and she goes on: "What a deep philosophy! - what theory of the world has ever gone further than this? The evil is not the opposer of the good, but its *collaborateur* - the left hand of God, as the Good is His right. I don't think I ever saw anything which affected me much more than this (3000 years ago) - the king at his entrance into life is initiated into the belief that what *we* call the evil was the giver of life and power as well as the good" (p.96). Beset, as she believed she was, by assaults of the devil which would incapacitate her for the life's work she longed to do, the idea she found in this and other Egyptian representations, that evil also has its enhancing function, gave a release which she welcomed as wisdom. What oppressed her, whether from within or without, need not, ancient Egypt suggested, be conceived of merely as a wrecker: here, it seemed, was an insight into a subtler kind of piety.[11] It was a month after this visit to Abu Simbel that she sat by herself among the ruins of Karnak and there, as her diary records, God spoke to her again. The language that Egypt was beginning to speak to her through *its* gods translates itself into the voice of *her* god but indeed the two are near to being one and the same thing. "In Karnak", she writes, "I felt that their God was my God. In Ipsamboul I felt more *at home* perhaps, than in any place of worship I ever was in" (p.188).

The idea embodied in the relief and celebrated in the letters became an important one in all her thinking. For Florence Nightingale, as for Harriet Martineau, experience of ancient Egypt and study of its religious thought and symbols had a determining effect on the shaping of her own religious ideas. At the beginning of her diary for 1853 she wrote "I have remodelled my whole religious belief from beginning to end".[12] Soon after her return to England she had begun work on a book which she intended should set out the grounds of religious faith in a way acceptable to modern thought. She had in mind, particularly, intelligent working men of a type with which she had some acquaintance and who, she knew, were quite alienated by the traditional teaching of the churches. She took up the work again in 1859 and it was privately printed, with the title *Suggestions for Thought*.[13] It was never published but the heart of it is contained in two articles she wrote for *Fraser's Magazine* of May and July, 1873. The first one, "A 'Note' of Interrogation", is particularly informative about the views she had by then arrived at. Man has made great progress, she writes, in identifying and understanding the laws of the physical universe but has never devoted the same attention to the laws of the moral world. These laws derive from the "character" of God who is perfect and, because perfect, institutes and operates through law. God teaches man by means of the inexorable consequences which follow his actions but there is no question of suffering being inflicted for its own sake: "*Not so*: for under this and through this all is the river deeply flowing (the imperishable, never interrupted Nile), the warp upon which all this suffering is the woof, the 'still small voice' - which is the plan of God to bring each and all of us to perfection through mankind learning to create mankind by experience, learning by means of the invariable, the inexorable nature of these consequences". Evil is equated with error and, as such, is to be seen as an agent of the teaching by which mankind will, in her striking phrase, "create mankind". As the letters some twenty-five years earlier had put it: "The old Egyptians believed that out of good came forth evil, and out of evil came forth good; or as I should translate it, out of the well-ordered comes forth the inharmonious, the passionate; and out of disorder again order; and both are a benefit" (p.96). The abiding influence of thoughts stimulated in Egypt is clearly to be seen in all this and indeed the reference to the imperishable, never-interrupted Nile acknowledges it.

Egypt and Egyptian images contributed strikingly also to the conception of man's relations to God which formed with increasing firmness in Florence Nightingale's mind. The Osirides at Abu Simbel made a very great impression on her. She found in them "the sublimest expression of spiritual and intellectual repose" ever seen (p.104). There was a similar kind of sublimity in a head of Sethos (Seti I): "this head is the most wonderful ideal of sublime serenity and childlike trust and confidence I ever saw" (p.154). She tried to account for the quality she saw in these Egyptian faces which was so different from that she was familiar with in Christian images. Christian art depicts sin and suffering, she says, but the ancient Egyptians showed "the sinless soul, which has never left the bosom of its God" and which finds Him "as near in one spot of his creation as in another, which does not wait for another world to enjoy His presence". There is no asceticism in the Egyptian ideal for it will reject none of the gifts of the Father; there is no struggle, for the soul has never loved anything better than God; there is no need for hope for there is trust in the present as well as in the future; and (especially telling words from Florence Nightingale): "there is no resignation, for where evil is to give life as well as good, it is absurd to talk of resigning oneself to a benefit. Then it is love, not resignation".

A passage which illuminates the direction of her thinking particularly strikingly occurs in her letter of January 17th, 1850, from Abu Simbel. (The passage is not included in Settin's selection.) It refers to a figure of Rameses II depicted as entering the presence of a trinity of gods and she describes it as, to her mind: "the sublimest ideal of prayer that ever entered the mind of man to conceive". She goes on: "The [figure of] Rameses is that of a perfect intellectual and spiritual man, who feels his connection with that God, whose first and last lesson through His Christ has been 'Be *one with* me', not be my instrument, nor my worshipper, nor my petitioner, but *one* with me. I am glad to have seen that representation of prayer, it has taught me more than all the sermons I ever read".[14] From the serenity and confidence she saw on the old Egyptian faces she derived the lesson that to preach abasement of the human before the divine is wrong: the relation between man and God is closer than that. She was not, unhappily, to attain in her own life the calm of spirit that Egypt suggested was not only a much-to-be-desired but also a possible ideal.

Like Harriet Martineau, Florence Nightingale found mental and spiritual stimulus and enlargement as she grew increasingly familiar with the relics of ancient Egypt and she could not understand how anyone could take a visit to these sites casually. "One wonders that people come back from Egypt and live lives as they did before", she writes (p.77). The remark applied specifically to the vanity of human aspirations, as she contemplated the mighty ruins of Karnak,[15] but it had relevance to smaller things as well as greater. Even on the Nile she could not escape the social duties which so plagued her at home, and night after night visitors came to the boat and had to be entertained. "It is very hard", she comments, "to be all day by the deathbed of the greatest of your race, and to come home and talk about quails..." [they were shot in quantity, for food] (p.139). Like Harriet Martineau she deplored the insensibility of many visitors to what was around them but unlike her she had no mission to open their eyes and merely exclaimed in irritation, "What do people come to Egypt for?"

For herself, the whole experience provoked deep thought, not least the striking and unsettling contrast between Egypt's splendid past and its present degeneracy. In a letter written off Kenneh, late in December, she reflected seriously on large issues of progress and degeneration. Past and present are words which, she writes, to Europeans "generally present a cheerful view of things" (p.73) but in Egypt the words ring quite differently: here they evoke "all that you can conceive strange and painful". Four thousand years ago this nation possessed a high civilisation and was adept in philosophy, art and science. Its religion was so enlightened as to inculcate worship of the one God and to conceive of a progression through eternity. Its philosophy was "so deep that all which Solomon knew of legislation, all that Pythagoras and Plato guessed of ethics and spiritual theories, seems to have been borrowed from them" (p.74). It was above all "a nation so spiritualised that death was to them more interesting than life: or rather death, as they put it, did not differ from life; life was so small a fragment of the whole to them, that the whole became of course of immeasurably more consequence".[16] Why after such development there should follow a terrible lapse is a question which greatly exercised her. To her, as to nineteenth century philosophy, it was a dominant concern to identify the laws which underlay human history, interpreted by her as the laws of God. The fall of a nation from high civilization to abject wretchedness must stem from the violation of some divine rule: must all nations follow Egypt's path or will some nation one day recognize the laws of God and obey them and so never lapse from its upward path of progress? Her insistence on the necessity of identifying fundamental laws and then obeying them is characteristic of her thought, as effectively illustrated by the use she would later make of the principle in relation to medical hygiene.

The passage as a whole carries also, however, a number of Martineau motifs: comparisons with the civilization of her own time and questioning of contemporary assumptions about such matters as the date of the creation of man, the notion of progress through history, the relation of life to death. The impact of Egypt stirred Florence Nightingale, as it stirred Harriet Martineau, to probe into her own mind and bring to light thoughts probably never expressed, even if consciously defined, before. The Egyptian journey came at a turbulent period in her inner life and the letters, for all their reticence, are a remarkable brew of seething thought and feeling as powerful external stimulus played upon an exacerbated internal situation. God and the devil both spoke to Florence Nightingale in Egypt and what they said is recorded in the letters.

(iii)

The circle of family and friends who first read them as they arrived through the post had no means of knowing what the letters omitted and so were not in a position to understand the significance of much that they contained. They were letters to be talked over, displayed and admired for their wit and the brilliance of their anecdotage and description. Florence Nightingale took care to provide for the entertainment of her audience as, for example, in her accounts of the innumerable winged, stinging or biting fellow-inhabitants of her boat. Other travellers might feel themselves persecuted beyond endurance by these alien hordes but they give Florence Nightingale the occasion for passages of lively and light-hearted wit. These are qualities which, despite the tensions underlying the letters, are in evidence often enough to reveal that as well as the sombre elements there was also an attractive and sociable aspect of her nature. Her funniest passages frequently depend on an interchange between human and animal - or insect - natures. Describing, for instance, how she tries to protect herself from the attacks of gnats, she tells how she shuts her cabin windows before sundown to keep as many as possible out but then she hears those who are already in "furling their wings and uttering little infernal cries of triumph". The whole episode is described as a battle of wits with each party trying to outmanoeuvre the other and ends with a confession that some gnats do succeed in getting inside her Levinge in spite of all her efforts; but "they have either sub-terranean passages or latch keys" (pp.25-26). Her account of visiting the interior of the Great Pyramid is an extended set-piece in which the human beings (herself included) become rats crawling through drains and it culminates in a scene of high comedy as she is hauled out, bonnetless, shoeless and undignified, to face the curious gaze of three grave Turks and their fifty-woman harem (pp.180-81). To describe the weariness of her party after a day's sightseeing, she writes that in the evening they "are all hung up by the tails, like the chameleons, pretending to be dead" (p.137). Even the elements acquire an anthropomorphic life: "The last night a storm arose, and we were obliged to anchor; but rain - three drops! - fell, and the wind was so terrified that it fainted away" (p.168). Her gift for striking phrases is evident throughout the letters but in passages of familiar anecdotage such as these the sparkle of her humour offers a welcome sight of her in relaxed mood, enjoying the exercise of her wit, often at her own expense but on these occasions without harshness.

In less light-hearted moments, the immediate and contemporary was a matter of serious, even grim, contemplation. For Florence Nightingale, as for Harriet Martineau, contact with and respect for another civilization sharpened awareness of shortcomings in her own society. The ancient Egyptian church allowed office and vocation in the church to women as, she observes, does every other church but the Anglican; and, in notable contrast to the English way, the Egyptians equated knowledge, including scientific knowledge, with holiness, so that "the very professing of it consecrated a man", an Isaac Newton as much as a St. Augustine (p.161). The spiritual and intellectual teacher was pre-eminent in the ancient society, a very different state of affairs from the situation in England which she deplores in depressingly familiar terms: at home, she writes, the schoolmaster's vocation is considered, "inconceivable as it sounds, almost *infra dig*" (p.136). In time the Egyptian priesthood degenerated into priestcraft but priestcraft, she writes, is all that modern England acknowledges and knows. She attended a bad sermon on Palm Sunday, 1850, in Cairo and the memory evidently recurs when she is summarizing, a little later, the characteristics of different religions as she sees them. The Egyptian is philosophical, the Roman Catholic spiritual, the Muslim imaginative, and the Protestant moral, but beyond that, she adds, "nothing else". As in the Gothic arch, "diminishing and diminishing and diminishing, line within line, and again within line", she saw the hand of man, reducing the Almighty to his own stature, so she heard the preacher, "diminishing the thought of God, and adding precept within precept, till he has twaddled it all away with his nineteenthly and his twentiethly" (p.192). Islamic architecture appealed to her strongly and, though she had no time for Mahomet, she admired some aspects of Muslim practice. In the mosques at Cairo it was pleasant to see that any man was welcome at any time: "Here the homeless find a home, the weary repose, the busy leisure, - if I could have said where any *woman* might go for an hour's rest, to me the feeling would have been perfect" (pp.27-28). The mosque seemed to her to be a better place of worship than St. Paul's though not perhaps than St. Peter's. Though men made baskets there and told each other stories as well as praying - or going to sleep - she was in no way upset by this: to her mind there was more real irreverence to be found in the behaviour of respectable congregations in London churches. Christians who mock at the Muslim's absorption in his prayers have little right to do so, she admonished. They should rather note with shame the care with which the Muslim studies his religion: he is commonly much better instructed in his faith, she remarks, than the average Christian is in his.

Some of Florence Nightingale's exercises in comparative religion are the product of earnest thought on issues which touch her nearly but there are others in which contrast between familiar and unfamiliar serves primarily as a means of attack on home-grown antipathies. Similarly acquaintance with the life and thought of ancient Egypt genuinely enlarged her outlook but could also be used for caustic comment on contemporary habits. In any comparison between *modern* Egypt and nineteenth century British society there was, however, no question but that whatever the faults of England they were as nothing compared with the squalor of modern Egypt and Egyptians. In one point only did the native peoples have an advantage - that is, in certain physical aptitudes. Like Harriet Martineau, Florence Nightingale was fascinated and excited by the muscular power and consummate skills exhibited by the Arabs who steered and hauled their boats through the dangerous waters of the cataracts and both drew a contrast between the intellectualized but physically under-educated society they were used to and what Florence Nightingale calls "the most wonderful development of instinct I suppose the world contains" (p.90).

Her description of the ascent of the cataract is vivid and dramatic and full of admiration for the men who accomplished it but her account of another aquatic episode strikes a very different note. This occurs quite early in the journey when the behaviour of one of the crew rouses the curiosity of the English company. Then they see, swimming towards the boat, "what looked like a line of the archbishop's rats" (p.50). As they near the boat, a mock-fight develops between these "black objects" and one of the crew-men: he is a Christian and these are fellow Christians, Coptic monks coming to beg alms. They open their mouths and he puts money under each tongue - it is like a parody of the taking of a sacramental wafer, though Florence Nightingale refrains from saying so - whereupon the monks swim off. When she observes the position of their monastery, "high on the cliffs of an impassable desert, and overlooking the valley of the dark and solemn Nile", she is disappointed and disgusted that a place fit for missionaries and ascetics should instead be given over to "these wretched aquatic beggars" (p.51).[17]

The Copts, however, "can hardly be considered as Christians" (p.71). This remark, from a different context, points to another element present in the retailing of the anecdote. To describe the swimming monks seen from the deck of the boat as rats and "black objects", may not, on its own, be something to be taken too seriously; but in fact the dehumanizing phraseology used here does not stand on its own. It seems that for much of the time Florence Nightingale could hardly consider modern Egyptians to qualify as human beings, let alone as Christians. Her choice of language on occasions is, at the least, disconcerting. In Assuan her visit coincided with that of a party of traders passing through with skins and slaves: "The skins were heaped up under the palms, and so were the slaves, most of them girls of about ten or fifteen, with beautiful little hands..." (p.88). Florence Nightingale and friends had earlier passed a crammed boatful of human cargo consisting of half-naked women and as they returned from an evening walk through the town they came upon the women again, sitting round a fire: "they came out to beg of us, and, in the dusk, looked like skulls, with their white teeth; they set up a horrid laugh when we gave them nothing, our guide poked one with his stick, when it was sitting down, as if it were a frog". In the same letter (p.87) she writes of children at Elephantine, "their black skins all dim and grimed with sand, like dusty tables, their dirty hair plaited in rats' tails, close to their heads...I heard some stones fall into the river, and hoped it was they, and that that debased life had finished..." Even when the physical condition of the children is better, their human status in her eyes is doubtful: "lairs of families...nests of little naked children (like nests of young foxes)...baying like jackals...things which looked about four months, climbing about like lizards..." (p.112). The persistent reduction of human beings to lower life forms and the attitude it betrays is the obverse of the comic vision which treats people and gnats and chameleons as a community of equals. The effect on the one hand is enlivening; on the other distressing.

Very early after her arrival in Egypt Florence Nightingale had been troubled by the condition of the people: "Oh, if one could either forget or believe, that the people here were one's fellow creatures, what a country this would be!" (p.41). If she were a Pharaoh, she writes later, returning to the body after three thousand years in the kingdom of the dead, she would choose to be an Arab and "come back to help these poor people" (p.134). She is well aware of the corruption of government and the "deep, grinding brutalising misery" but instinctively she recoils from the victims. There is not only physical squalor but moral degradation among the natives who live in the ruins of Luxor temple: "I never before saw any of my fellow-creatures degraded...but I longed to have intercourse with them, to stay with them, and make plans for them; but here, one gathered one's clothes about one, and felt as if one had trodden on a nest of reptiles" (p.81). Yet, "they are such an attaching race, the poor Arabs", she writes on another occasion, moved by the tears of the crew as they parted at the end of the journey. In relation to the inhabitants, as to other aspects of the country, the contradictions of Egypt unsettled her and her mood, deeply disturbed in any event, swung from disgust and hatred of sites and people to appreciation of the beauties and attractions of both and to wonder and excitement at being in the land of "the greatest race, perhaps, that ever existed" (p.152). Years, later, Benjamin Jowett, a much valued friend, accused her of exaggeration and certainly the letters show her dealing freely in superlatives. She was not a placid character and no half-way house could contain her.

Once emancipated from her family and gone to the Crimea, Florence Nightingale focused intense and effective attention on army welfare. She became devoted to the men - her children she called them - and fought thereafter with all her strength to secure dignity and proper attention for the common soldier. Yet great as was her humanity on this scale, in personal matters, as her biographer Cecil Woodham-Smith writes, there was "something about Florence which chilled".[18] Mrs Gaskell similarly identified in her a want of love for individuals which went together with utterly unstinting and unselfish love for mankind at large.[19] Her attitude to the children in Egypt whom she thought would be better drowned and her use of "it" to denote one of the female slaves point not merely to a lack of humanity but to a certain ruthlessness. It may have been part of the equipment which enabled her to do her greater service to humanity and to channel her energies to such extraordinary effect.

Harriet Martineau, large and influential figure as she was, lacked the final touch of greatness and knew that this was so. Her sensitivity to the individual, however, gave depth and force to the campaigns which she fought with all her mind and heart. One of these was for individual freedom and the right to develop whatever faculties the individual had. Egyptian harems denied both and were to her the grossest offence. She studied with care and sympathy the individual women she met on her visits and what she has to say about the harems is suffused with pity and indignation on their behalf. Florence Nightingale also visited a harem; her tone, however, is different. She was relieved that, rather than rousing disgust, the Pasha's wife, "our hareem specimen" (p.208), was beautiful, well-bred and gracious. Like Harriet Martineau, she was oppressed by the sheer boredom of the empty, enclosed life: "Oh, the *ennui* of that magnificent palace, it will stand in my memory as a circle of hell!" The visit was a penance and she was glad to have a reason for not staying long but, clear as she was as to the horror of the place, she remained detached, not, like her predecessor, imagining deeply and with personal pain what it must be to be condemned to live a life by that system. It might be thought that, chafing as she was at her own restricted life, she would feel some particular sympathy with the harem women but she gives no sign of it. They are evidently too alien for any connection to be made.

The situation of Muslim women had come home quite sharply to her on an earlier occasion when she was personally involved. This occurred in Alexandria, soon after her arrival in Egypt. She felt a compelling curiosity to see the inside of a Muslim place of worship and one of her fellow-countrymen "good-naturedly" (p.26) arranged for her to do so, though for a European woman to enter a mosque was unprecedented and gravely offensive. She was obliged to dress in full Egyptian fashion, completely enveloped and veiled in the orthodox manner, and needed to take great care not to show her hands which would betray her. There was a risk of serious disturbance if the masquerade were to be discovered by the Muslims but, in spite of crowding round, they failed to recognize the infidels in their midst. Florence Nightingale found it a horrifying experience: "I felt so degraded, knowing what they took us for, what they felt towards us...That quarter of an hour seemed to reveal to one what it is to be a woman in these countries, where Christ has not been to raise us. God save them, for it is a hopeless life". She remained calm enough to make her observations of what was going on about her, however, and even to report that "the mosque struck me with a pleasant feeling". It is difficult for a modern reader to avoid some distaste at the whole episode. The determination displayed may perhaps be admirable but the willingness to undertake an elaborate charade to deceive the Muslims and violate their holy place strikes with the chill Mrs Woodham-Smith speaks of.[20] Back in Cairo at the end of the journey Florence Nightingale visited more mosques with considerable appreciation of their beauty and also of what they offered to their devout. Cairo was not so fanatic as Alexandria so she did not need to go in disguise but the people were still likely to get irritated by her presence and on one occasion the native attendant had to protect the party with his whip. The retreat, she says, was like backing out of a field where there are angry cows. Her comments are ambivalent as they often are when the native population is in question. She expresses sympathy with "Mahometan horror" (p.197) at her presence in their sacred mosque but this goes with deep humiliation at exciting it in the breasts of people to whom she cannot refrain from applying animal imagery.

Strong characters are unlikely to be consistently easy company, a truism as applicable to Florence Nightingale as to Harriet Martineau, though the rough and smooth of their temperaments fell in different places. Florence Nightingale was a complex character called to a remarkable destiny and exerting in the fulfilment of it what might be supposed to be incredible powers of mind and discipline of body. It is hardly possible in considering her to go beyond Mrs Gaskell's summary remark: "she is really so extraordinary a creature that anything like a judgement of her must be presumptuous".[21] Her Egyptian journey is a very minor episode in her career but not a negligible one. It throws light forward on to what she afterwards did and became and it contributes to the history of the impact of Egypt on nineteenth-century minds and sensitivities. The letters give glimpses into deep but not still waters, agitated by strong emotions and also by urgent and sometimes tormented probing into the nature of life and the duties of the living. They present a personality given to quick impressions sharply registered which mask, to some degree, the profounder movements taking place below. These energies, criss-crossing in Egypt, later found their direction and their release and created the force that became Florence Nightingale, a woman who was far more than 'the lady with the lamp' and to whom, in olden times, a temple could worthily have been built. Egypt was a precipitating agent. At the beginning she was, naturally enough, more comfortable in European Italy but it was the very alien-ness of Egypt and its ancient culture which acted upon her, as upon other intelligent and sensitive minds, and led to fresh and critical awareness of old assumptions and to the opening of new intellectual and spiritual horizons. In departing she wrote of it as a country which, "like its own old Nile, has overflowed and fertilised the world" (p.188). It quickened things in her too and the deposit from her Egyptian experience formed a not inconsiderable part of the soil in which the commanding growth of her later years was to occur. In 1853 the Crimean War broke out and Florence Nightingale, prepared by an often harsh discipline, entered history.

Chapter III

Amelia Edwards:
"Four persons might sit in it...and play a rubber comfortably"

(i)

Of the three women with whom this book is concerned, Amelia Edwards is the only one whose name is particularly associated with Egypt. Harriet Martineau wrote a substantial book about her Middle Eastern journey and her experiences in Egypt left a lasting impress upon her thinking thereafter; but her activities spread widely through most areas of nineteenth century life and, crucial as Egypt was, it had to take a place alongside much else in a long and active career. Biographers have treated Florence Nightingale's visit to Egypt as a very minor episode in a life which later acquired historic dimensions - this is understandable enough though in doing so they have failed to see how strikingly her letters and the diary she kept at the time illuminate the psychological and spiritual forces which impelled her in her later career. Amelia Edwards is a much less familiar figure than these others. She was well-known in her day, particularly as a novelist, but until the recent publication of a paperback edition of her book *A Thousand Miles up the Nile*,[1] she was generally forgotten after her death in 1892. In one area, however, she has never been forgotten. *A Thousand Miles up the Nile* is an attractive, entertaining and informative book and whets curiosity about the woman who wrote it. It is also a pivotal work in the author's career. It registers the impact of Egypt just as *Eastern Life* and Florence Nightingale's *Letters from Egypt* do but Amelia Edwards did not return from her journey as the others did, to resume the life she had led before. Instead she abandoned other activities to devote herself exclusively to working for the proper excavation and recording of the Egyptian monuments. So decisive was the influence of Egypt that the journey up the Nile changed the whole direction of her life and her contribution to modern Egyptology is honoured by all who work in that field.

It is ironic that her going to Egypt at all was quite unpremeditated and almost accidental. She and a friend, a Miss Renshawe, had begun a sketching tour of France but were so frustrated by unremitting rain that they decided to go somewhere else for the sake of the sun. They chose Cairo more or less by whim and set out without plans or preparation. Once there, Amelia Edwards was commissioned to write a book, for she had written travel books before, and so she hired a dahabieh and embarked on the journey that was to redirect her life. It was November 29th, 1873, when she arrived in Cairo. She was forty-two years old, just a few years younger than Harriet Martineau had been when she also made the journey. Like her she had never married though also like her she had once been engaged. This episode, in common with much else in her private history, is obscure but it appears that she broke off the engagement on the grounds that the regard and esteem she felt for the gentleman was not enough for marriage. Neither she nor Harriet Martineau seems to have had much natural enthusiasm for the married state. Both valued the freedom of action which independence gave them and the conditions of a conventional marriage were likely to have had little appeal for either of them. Something of Amelia Edwards's views is hinted in the number of times she applies the reductive adjective "little" to the wives who appear in her writing - the "Little Lady" who is part of the company in *A Thousand Miles up the Nile* has several diminutive companions elsewhere. Her own fiction is certainly not "ladylike" in the traditional sense, for novels and short stories alike range in location and sensation far beyond the "littleness" of the domestic sphere. Plot and characterization tend to be weak but the variety of settings and activities covered (engine-driving and lion-taming among them) is remarkable. It is possible that there is another story behind Amelia Edwards's spinsterhood, some episode of personal life perhaps, which put marriage out of sight, but if so, no record of it remains.

Like Harriet Martineau again, Amelia Edwards was a prolific professional writer, depending on her pen for her livelihood. Both were strong women but, a few parallelisms apart, in character and circumstance there was little in common between them. Amelia Edwards was the daughter of a half-pay army officer, who had seen service under Wellington in the Peninsular War, and an Irish mother who was descended from the Walpoles and the Fitzgeralds. The mother was, it appears, a clever and vivacious woman and it was probably to her that her daughter owed her wit and her sharp intelligence and liveliness of mind.[2] However this may be, the young Amelia was undoubtedly a very gifted child. She began to write at a tender age but she went on to make a serious study of music and planned to make that her career, perhaps as an opera singer for she had a good voice and was devoted to the theatre. From early on she showed a considerable talent for art also, something to which her travel books, illustrated by herself, bear witness. In the end she settled on literature as her means to independence and columns of the British Library catalogue testify to her industry and also to her contemporary success. Her original work included a volume of ballads, many short stories and eight novels, several of which went into multiple editions and were widely translated. Matthew Arnold and Browning, among others, wrote flatteringly to her about them. She contributed regularly to Dickens's periodicals and was much in demand as a journalist, claiming that she had done every kind of newspaper work except parliamentary debates and police reports. She compiled anthologies of poetry and put together histories of France and of England. This was hack work, part of the working life of a marketable writer, but it contributed valuably to the wide reading and the impressive range of information which she had at her command and which enriched her original work.

Her parents died within a week of each other in 1860 and four years later she left London and moved to Westbury-on-Trym, a village near Bristol. The adjoining house still stands but Amelia Edwards's property, The Larches, 22 Eastfield, was destroyed during the second world war. There she lived for the rest of her life with periodic visits to London. It was a reclusive life, shared only by her friend, Mrs Ellen Braysher, a widow nearly thirty years older than herself. Their acquaintance had probably been formed in London days when Mrs Braysher lived among a circle of lively and distinguished friends, including at one time the actor William

McCready.[3] A Braysher daughter died in 1864 and this may have prompted the bereaved mother and her younger friend (almost a daughter) to set up house together. One of Amelia Edwards's letters preserved among the Egypt Exploration Society archives gives a glimpse of the relationship as it was in later years. The letter is dated from Westbury, May 4th, 1884, and addressed to R.S. Poole of the British Museum. The background is the indignation, widely felt, at Gladstone's delay in sending help to Gordon at Khartoum: "Old ladies and babies are bound to be vegetables", Amelia Edwards writes. "My old lady is a most rampaging, vehement, political, belligerent, Gladstone-hating boiling-over vegetable - quite uncontrollable and unmanageable. But in truth," she goes on, "she and I are both heart-sick and exhausted with indignation and impatience and shame at the whole Gordon-Khartoum affair". The references to Mrs Braysher are amused and affectionate and the style is characteristic of Amelia Edwards but in effect little is revealed about the day-to-day situation of sharing life with a much older companion whose health in the natural course of things deteriorated with age.

Various more or less picturesque details of daily life in Westbury are included in autobiographical notes which Amelia Edwards provided from time to time at the request of her admiring readers.[4] She writes about her routine daily walks around her garden and about her treasured collection of books with the grace and charm and humour which characterize her but, despite the apparent candour and air of friendly ease with which she addresses her audience, she preserves here as elsewhere, in relation to more intimately personal matters, a deep well of reserve. Undoubtedly her life was extremely busy, at first with supplying the publishers' material by which she earned her living and then, when she came back from Egypt, with the work she undertook to promote expert excavation and recording of the ancient remains. Shocked by the neglect of the monuments and the uncontrolled looting which was taking place, she, in alliance with others, founded the Egypt Exploration Fund (later the Egypt Exploration Society) and became its first Secretary. "Her energy, enthusiasm and zeal brought about the foundation of the Egypt Exploration Fund in 1882", a distinguished contemporary wrote, "and for some years it owed its success entirely to her tact and work and extraordinary power of organisation".[5] In the service of ancient Egypt she gave up all her other writing and worked herself to exhaustion in attempts to raise support and money, to encourage research and to mollify as far as she could the competing vanities and special interests put in play when Egyptology became a sphere in which reputations, as well as precious relics, could be won or lost. The rediscovery of Egypt and the advances of knowledge during the nineteenth century make a thrilling story but it is also a rough one of jealousies, underhand deals and knives in the back as national, international and personal interests fought each other with the usual mixture of honourable and dishonourable motives. Amelia Edwards, toiling at her desk in Westbury, never lost sight of the goal and kept clear of faction, though she used all her influence to support Flinders Petrie in whom she recognized - as not all her colleagues did - an archaeologist of genius.

When she died, she bequeathed nearly £5000 to University College, London, for the founding of a professorship in Egyptian Archaeology and Philology. This was the first Chair of Egyptology to be established in any British University and she intended it should be occupied by Petrie. The provisions of her will were carefully designed to exclude competing claims and in acknowledgment of her wishes Petrie was duly appointed. The books and antiquities which she also left to University College were housed in a specially designated and equipped room, now called the Edwards Library. When, in 1992 the College published a history of the Department to mark the centenary of its founding (*The First Hundred Years. Egyptology at University College London 1892-1992,* by Rosalind M. Janssen) they chose, very properly, a portrait bust of Amelia Edwards to preside over the volume.

In 1889-90 she undertook an extensive lecture tour of the United States, partly to eke out her own finances, which were never large (a Civil List pension was awarded to her a few months before she died) but principally to build up American support for the Fund.[6] She was an effective speaker and made a great impression with her combination of personal charm and professional authority. In the course of the tour, unfortunately, she fell and broke her arm and, though she insisted on fulfilling her schedule regardless, the accident combined with the very demanding programme was to weaken her health. She died in 1892 as a result of influenza contracted while supervising the unloading and despatch of antiquities at Millwall Docks. She had given most of the last twenty years of her life to Egypt and it was appropriate that she should die, though sadly early, in its service. She is buried in the churchyard at Henbury, a village adjacent to Westbury - why not Westbury itself can only be guessed. The grave is marked by an obelisk, recording Amelia Edwards's own death and those of Emma Braysher and her daughter, and also by an ankh, the Egyptian sign of life. The obelisk had by that time become anglicized but the ankh may have been a too blatantly non-Christian symbol for the vicar of her own parish to accept. That Amelia Edwards insisted on it speaks clearly of her own estimate of the respect due not only to the works but also to the ideals of ancient Egypt.

Her charm, wit, and talent as an entertaining and sympathetic companion are recurrent motifs in accounts of her but the deeper layers of her character remain hidden. Matilda Betham-Edwards, her cousin, ascribes to her what she somewhat ominously calls "the perilous dower of personal fascination" and goes on, with tantalizing vagueness: "No one ever exerted stronger influence, and it was hardly her fault if she at times awakened interest or affection she could not return". Kate Bradbury, who assisted Amelia Edwards with Fund business, wrote to Petrie to inform him of the death and provokes equally unanswerable questions about the nature of the experiences and the emotions which lay behind the exterior: "Amy had for you a private affection", she wrote, "- and she does not love many people for all her seeming geniality. She once enumerated to me the two or three people for whom she 'cared' - and of you she said 'And I am fond of Petrie - though I might just as well be fond of a young obelisk'".[7] These comments suggest a cool personality which does not offer or seek close relationships but they and the reclusive life in Westbury and the devotion to unceasing hard work may be equally suggestive of banked-down fires. Her cousin draws a picture of a vital, assertive and confident young girl with energies which often ran over conventional bounds. Some particular experience, perhaps, or a frustrating sense of the restricted prospects open to an energetic, talented, ambitious woman, without social status or money, may have led her to direct her energies and pour all her hope for self-fulfilment into one intellectual and artistic channel and one quasi-filial emotional outlet.

(ii)

One of her novels gives some substance to this reading of her. On the whole Amelia Edwards's novels have been fairly discarded. She shows at all times a gift for scenery and portrays a scene with a keen eye for detail and a relish of dramatic possibility but characterization and plot are hardly gripping or convincing. Her book describing her mountaineering in the Dolomites, *Untrodden Peaks and Unfrequented Valleys* (1873) shows her amply endowed with physical toughness and courage and the novels have their daring too, in such sensational episodes as an English lord faking his own death and transforming himself into an Italian sailor, an eruption of Vesuvius, and a robust blockade-running incident in the American Civil Wars. None of them is so daring, however, as *Hand and Glove*, published in 1858, though it is not physical adventurousness that is in question here.

The plot focuses on the character of the man who is intro-duced as the Reverend Alexis Xavier Hamel. Amelia Edwards's novels frequently owe something to distinguished contempor-aries, especially Dickens and the Brontes, but it is Byron and the Byronic hero who exert a potent influence on *Hand and Glove*. The choice itself is an interesting one but even more interesting is the fact that, as well as his Byronic qualities, there are aspects of Hamel which appear to derive from no-one else but his author and it is these which give the book its particular value. *Hand and Glove* was one of Amelia Edwards's first novels and in it she gives expression to elements of her private self which she later took care to conceal from public gaze. When Hamel comes upon the scene he is in his forties, a strikingly handsome man conveying an impres-sion of power both of intellect and character. His previous career is not revealed till towards the end of the book when it is discovered that as a young man he had been one of the principal actors in a scheme to promote investment in a bogus diamond-mining company. He had made off with his substantial ill-gotten gains to South America leaving hundreds of dupes financially ruined behind him. He had been caught and sentenced to penal servitude in the mines but had escaped and made his way to Vienna where he had posed as a French nobleman. Exposed there as an impostor, he toured other fashionable continental resorts, took to gambling and won and lost fortunes. He was caught cheating and retreated to Venice where he became a professional singer. Failing to make a fortune there, his next rôle was as tutor to a young Englishman travelling abroad. By this time he had developed some inclination to live more quietly and become respectable, to which end he presented himself as a clergyman. He forfeited his post, however, and the chance of a good living by rashly introducing his young pupil to gambling. At this ebb he has been glad to accept appointment to the small Protestant community in the town of Chalons-sur-Saône. There he falls in love with the very young and very innocent Marguerite and is on the point of marrying her when someone from his past recognizes him and unmasks him by tearing the glove from his right hand and thereby bringing to view the convict's brand burned into it.

In outline this looks tawdry enough but there are some unexpected features of Amelia Edwards's treatment of Hamel. Most striking is the account of the sermon he delivers to his new parishioners. He gives them a history of Christianity but it is a history presented as an unrelieved sequence of oppression, tyranny, persecution and destruction. All the violence and suffering have been inflicted allegedly in the cause of saving souls but in fact souls have not been saved, Christianity has not triumphed. The message, several times repeated, is "Despair...There is no hope in the face of these things, for where there is salvation for one, and perdition for ten thousand, there is woe for all!'" Amelia Edwards gives the substance of Hamel's sermon with the same surging eloquence with which she says he delivered it, adding that extensive reading and keen judgement gave foundation to the passion of his utterance. No attempt is made to rebut this highly unorthodox and astonishing sermon: on the contrary, Gartha, the first person narrator and the voice of sound sense and intelligence in the novel, remarks that she can never forget it.

76

At a later stage it transpires that Hamel has unconventional ideas about literature as well as about religion. Talking to Marguerite, he refutes the common judgement that novels are trivial and unworthy of serious attention. They are valuable teachers of young and old, he says, and, "More than this, a good novel is a work of art, and as deathless as a canto of Tasso, or a statue of Michaelangelo". These claims for the high artistic status of the novel were unusual in their time (and much later) but in the present context the most interesting part of Hamel's mini-lecture is what follows. The pre-eminently valuable and lasting achievement of the novel, he argues, is to provide a record of contemporary life and manners so that the future may see the men and women of the past as they lived and breathed. How much better if Petrarch and Spenser had written novels instead of sonnets and *The Faerie Queene*! In expressing these views there is no doubt that Hamel speaks for his creator. In an article entitled 'On being a Novelist', Amelia Edwards writes of the high value she put on the recording function of the novelist and of how much she esteemed Trollope among her contemporaries for his achievements in this kind. The stress she puts on the value of records which will enable the past to be brought to life again in the future evidently corresponds to some deep-seated psychological urge. It will be a driving force throughout her life, translated in later years into devoted care for the preservation and interpretation of the remote past of Egyptian antiquity. The strong impulse to secure resurrection in these terms perhaps had some connection with the religious scepticism which Hamel's sermon suggests.

Hamel is described throughout as brilliant and fascinating, "fascinating" being the word repeated over and over again. Amelia Edwards herself is clearly strongly attracted by him. The sexual element in this author-character situation is particularly obvious in an episode in which Marguerite and Gartha are the unseen witnesses of Hamel's brutal subjugation of his dog in order to bring it to cringing obedience. The incident uncannily anticipates the scene in D.H. Lawrence's *Women in Love* when Gerald Crich asserts his mastery over the frightened mare at a level crossing. The *Hand and Glove* version stands out all the more for being quite unrelated to any significant development in the plot. This novel, in fact, seems to signal unmistakably that beneath the poised and gracious exterior of its author there are wilder elements, unorthodox ideas and at least the potentiality of passion. Religion does not become an issue in her other novels, though there is morality aplenty as the market required; and there is no other Hamel. Amelia Edwards became circumspect but the energies glimpsed in *Hand and Glove* go some way towards explaining her capacity for total commitment, as when she dedicated her strength and her talents to the cause of ancient Egypt. They account also for the impression her books make that hers was not only a much-gifted and engaging personality but one with hidden depths. The bizarre, the melodramatic and the supernatural figure in much of her writing and were evidently active elements in her imaginative world. *A Thousand Miles up the Nile* presents a serene surface but still waters proverbially run deep and it would be rash to assume that all was placid in her temperament. The controlled and confident persona on public display may well have been subject to some self-censorship: if so, the result composed from the acceptable elements is an undoubtedly successful blend of keen intelligence, lively wit and good manners. *A Thousand Miles up the Nile*, in particular, offers its readers the very attractive company of an entertaining, good-humoured companion, a cultivated woman with a well-stocked mind who wears her learning lightly, is always mindful of the comfort of her audience but never falls into the superficial or the patronizing.

(iii)

It was not an achievement that came out of the blue. All her previous writing had prepared for it and when later she had become fully immersed in Egyptology and was a frequent contributor to specialist journals she was not shy of claiming that she had the advantage of gifts which more professional scholars in the field lacked. "I am the only romanticist in the world who is also an Egyptologist", she wrote. Others had never, she said, done as she had, "flung themselves into the life and love of imaginary men and women; they have never studied the landscape painting of scenery in words". She alone among them knew how to write "a picturesque and popular style", for she had specially cultivated it, "worked at it as if it were a science - and mastered it...style is an instrument which I have practised sedulously, and which I can plan upon".[8] These are revealing words and entirely relevant to *A Thousand Miles*. For all its easy manners, the book is a deliberately constructed piece of work, drawing on all the presentational skills its author had acquired in some thirty years of energetic and successful writing. She had learnt to handle character and dialogue and to describe scenery effectively and evocatively and she had learnt how to create a tone, assured and assuring but neither bullying nor soporific. The style is far from being the unsophisticated expression of the woman any more than "The Writer" as she appears in the book is to be taken as a complete representation of the woman who wrote. A character emerges, nevertheless, equivocal in some respects but even in its evasions distinct, well-marked and eminently capable of rousing interest and curiosity.

It was Harriet Martineau's way to engage head-on with controversial issues but that was not Amelia Edwards's style. She was, for example, an active supporter of the movement for the emancipation of women and Vice-President of the Society for Promoting Women's Suffrage but she was not one of the movement's conspicuous heroines. The novels, with their young women who become art students or wage-earners and who insist on mutual understanding and mutual respect in marriage, respond to feminist reading but they are not militant. The points once taken are seen to be forceful but they are never sharply obtruded. A comparatively overt expression of her sympathies comes in her defence and celebration of Queen Hatasu (Hatshepsut) in *Pharaohs, Fellahs and Explorers* when she is clearly indignant at the reluctance of scholars to recognize the status and achievements of this queen; but her position is well covered within the general scholarly context. She left her collection of Egyptian antiquities to the University of London, selecting that institution as the beneficiary because it was the only University in the United Kingdom at the time which admitted men and women on equal terms. Other legacies went to Somerville College, Oxford, a women's college. In such ways she signalled clearly but not obtrusively her views and sympathies.

Particularly striking is the absence, both from the lectures and from *A Thousand Miles*, of any discussion of the impact upon her of ancient Egyptian religion. Such discussion looms large in *Eastern Life* and in Florence Nightingale's letters - indeed Harriet Martineau believed it to be the principal matter of her book. An obvious conclusion would be that Amelia Edwards was indifferent to such topics except as a subject for scholarly investigation. *Hand and Glove*, however, shows that there was some fire in her thinking on these matters and Egyptian religious thought is said to have held a particular interest for her. Wallis Budge, writing of the long conversations she used to have with Dr Samuel Birch, Keeper of Oriental Antiquities in the British Museum, remarks: "I never met anyone who had so thoroughly absorbed the mystic and magical influence of Egypt past and present, and who could clothe the impressions which they make upon the mind in such well-fitting and expressive words."[9] It is not easy to guess at this special enthusiasm from what she writes. Amelia Edwards did not wear her heart on her sleeve nor display all her mind to the public. If she felt a natural distaste for self-exposure, her reserve would have been fortified by the fact that she wrote for her living and, later, in order to gather support for the Fund. Of necessity she had to have careful regard to her audience. By the age of forty she had established herself as novelist and journalist but she did not occupy the influential position of Harriet Martineau nor did she have the financial backing to enable her to take risks, as Miss Martineau did. Later when she wrote in the service of her Egyptian cause, prudence was still required so that potential supporters might not be alienated.

Her skilful handling of her audience is in evidence everywhere in *A Thousand Miles*. She offers a well-judged blend of informality, entertainment and information and her capacity to assess the proportions in which scholarship and lighter matter could successfully be mingled was one of her valuable gifts. She did not come to Egyptology till late and lacked the training of a professional scholar but she took the informative part of her book very seriously. Far from rushing into print when she came back from Egypt, she spent two years in confirming and extending her knowledge and taking pains to consult the best authorities. In the following years she developed her knowledge further and a revised edition of *A Thousand Miles* in 1889 came ballasted with footnotes correcting or bringing up-to-date the 1877 text. Her efforts were rewarded by the praise of experts and some idea of the standing she achieved in the Egyptological world is given by the fact that she was invited to read a paper at the Orientalist Congress in Vienna in 1885. In writing *A Thousand Miles*, however, she was addressing an audience composed largely of the home-bound and the indifferently informed and she faced the problem of which Harriet Martineau had been acutely aware: that of rousing in her readers the same eager interest in the ancient sites which she herself felt and of stretching their imaginations to envisage unfamiliar images and encompass ideas unprovided-for within their accustomed mental frames. Her solutions are different from Harriet Martineau's. Her natural mode is not impassioned rhetoric but leads her to quieter, more homely ground. Visiting the Serapeum at Sakkhara on the way up river, she and her party enter a chamber in which stands the enormous hieroglyphed sarcophagus of a sacred bull, dating from the XXVIth dynasty. To convey as graphically as possible the vast size of this object, Amelia Edwards uses a measure which she expects will impress her readers with immediate force: "Four persons", she writes, "might sit in it round a small card-table, and play a rubber comfortably" (p.57).

There are a good many such aids to the imagination in the earlier chapters of *A Thousand Miles*. The dimensions of the Great Pyramid, for example, are established by the calculation that it is higher than the cross on the top of St Paul's but not quite so high as Box Hill in Surrey; its area would a little more than cover Lincoln's Inn Fields. Such reassuring references, however, make only a small part of Amelia Edwards's repertoire of resources for ensuring that a willing band will follow her on the long mental and physical journey up the Nile. *A Thousand Miles* opens like a novel and lures the reader over the threshold at once. It might be the beginning of a detective story set, as many stories have been, in the old Shepheard's Hotel in Cairo with its collection of miscellaneous and sometimes mysterious guests of many types, nationalities and callings. "Two wandering Englishwomen" enter this scene and rouse speculation but they are, in fact, it is soon discovered, the writer herself and her friend. (The friend, Miss Renshawe, is referred to throughout the book only as 'L'). Mystery is not quite lost for their arrival is seen as something of the nature of a magical transportation, from rainy France to an awakening in a rose-coloured dawn with an enchanted garden outside the window: "and here where the garden was bounded by a high wall and a windowless house, I saw a veiled lady walking on the terraced roof in the midst of a cloud of pigeons" (p.3). This is enticing enough but there is to be no lingering. The scene changes to the native bazaars and all the vivid variety of life which throngs the narrow passages. One long sentence enumerates the types with relish and sympathy: "Here are Syrian dragomans in baggy trousers and braided jackets; barefooted Egyptian fellaheen in ragged blue shirts and felt skull-caps; Greeks in absurdly stiff white tunics, like walking pen-wipers; Persians with high mitre-like caps of dark woven stuff; swarthy Bedouins in flowing garments, creamy-white with chocolate stripes a foot wide, and head-shawl of the same bound about the brow with a fillet of camel's hair; Englishmen in palm-leaf hats and knickerbockers, dangling their long legs across almost invisible donkeys...blue-black Abyssinians with incredibly slender, bowed legs, like attenuated ebony balustrades; Armenian priests, looking exactly like Portia as the Doctor, in long black gowns and high square caps...merchants, beggars, soldiers, boat-men, labourers, workmen, in every variety of costume, and of every shade of complexion from fair to dark, from tawny to copper-colour, from deepest bronze to bluest black" (pp. 4-5). In its sharp sense of colour and its unexpected similes this is an early example of a typical Amelia Edwards scene. It is also an example of one of her favourite techniques, a bringing together of multiple activities in one long sentence so as to convey a sense of brimming and picturesque life.[10] The success of this technique depends, as well as on a sharp eye for detail and the inventiveness of her witty images, on her good ear for rhythmic structure in phrase and sentence. Amelia Edwards's verse is at best undistinguished but her prose is a versatile and well tuned instrument and she has a strong sense of cadence and of architectonics.

The broad canvas on which she has painted the market is shortly after put aside for miniature studies of individuals. An

Egyptian gentleman in European dress with a Turkish fez, driven by an English groom in an English phaeton passes: "Before him wand in hand, bare-legged, eager-eyed, in Greek skull-cap and gorgeous gold-embroidered waistcoat and fluttering white tunic, flies a native Sais, or running footman...The Sais (strong, light and beautiful, like John of Bologna's Mercury) are said to die young. The pace kills them" (p.6). The whole parade of the passing show is masterly, complete with its touch of shadow to set off the brilliance of life and colour. It is wound up by a train of camels "ill-tempered and supercilious, craning their scrannel necks above the crowd".

Amelia Edwards's painter's eye is naturally much engaged in passages of description and, as the passages quoted suggest, she is often most effective when there is movement. Another of her interests comes into prominence in scenes where there is not merely movement but dramatic action. Her cousin noted that she was much attracted by the theatre and certainly she had a penchant for dramatic - or melodramatic - scenes in her novels. The departure of a caravan for Mecca and a performance of howling dervishes, both taking place while she was in Cairo before embarking on her dahabieh, give her splendid opportunities to exercise her skill in scene setting and building up excitement. The dervishes' performance begins slowly and then bursts into convulsive, frenzied action. Amelia Edwards is fully equal to the dramatic demands of this, directing the pace of her narrative, bringing it to its fast and maddened climax and then allowing the terrifying energy to ebb away and normal life to reassert itself, with the spectacle of dervishes sitting on cane benches in the shade and sipping coffee. Her sense of the dramatic qualities in a scene and her talent for making the most of them are considerable assets in her account of her travels. The stimulus need not be by any means as sensational as the dervishes. Arriving at Derr in Nubia, her party finds the landing-place and town unexpectedly deserted. All at once a strange, wild and plaintive cry is heard and they become aware of a crowd of men standing on rising ground some distance away. These men are watching a real life performance in which the actors are all women. A funeral, accompanied by ceremonial dancing and chanting, is taking place. Its principal figure at first is a young woman who leads the mourners but later an old woman, the mother of the dead man, totters feebly towards the grave, stretches out her arms and laments till her grief overwhelms her and, "falling down in a sort of helpless heap, like a broken-hearted dog, she lay with her face to the ground, and there stayed" (pp. 250-1). The story is told with much sympathy but the theatrical inspiration which dictates the treatment is unmistakable and it imprints the scene sharply on the imagination. The English visitors are the audience who are gradually inducted into the meaning of what they are witnessing, the old men whom they first encounter, sitting silent and immobile outside the Governor's palace, are the dumb-show which prognosticates something solemn to follow, the men who watch the women are the stage audience and the mourners constitute the essential play which centres at last on the single figure of the old and desolated mother. It is a moving and very skilfully handled episode.

The crew, naturally, are part of the cast of characters which populate the book. They are described with sympathy but without the attempt to individualize them which Harriet Martineau made. There are also the travelling companions. At its largest the company consisted of Amelia Edwards herself and L; a painter whose object in travelling was to paint a big picture at Abu Simbel; a honeymoon pair whom she, with unconcealed irony, calls The Happy Couple; and a maid of whom, beyond noting her existence, nothing is said. The bridegroom is further identified as The Idle Man, a title whose sting is not entirely drawn by her explanation that "he has scholarship, delicate health, and leisure" (p.88). The bride, who makes several innocuous appearances, is The Little Lady. The Happy Couple's enthusiasm for temple haunting diminishes long before Amelia Edwards's and they hasten back to Cairo before completing the trip. With her characteristic desire to reduce the degree of intimacy with her readers - as distinct from companionableness - Amelia Edwards refers to herself most often, not in the first person, but as The Writer.

Of these companions Amelia Edwards clearly had the most respect for the painter. It is he who first discovers the remains of an hitherto unrecorded building at Abu Simbel which Amelia Edwards describes and comments on in careful, scholarly detail. It was a joy to her and a pride to have participated in so unexpected an archaeological find and on her return she plunged into eager research as to the history, function and significance of the building. This was one of the occasions when she turned to Birch for his opinion and guidance. The Painter comes well out of this episode as he does out of another, but this occasion, occurring earlier in the book, is treated, not seriously, but in a vein of ironic comedy, a style of which Amelia Edwards is a mistress. The Painter, who was perhaps not himself the most humorous of men, had spent some time compiling "a little vocabulary of choice Arab malediction" which he carried in his note-book to have handy if required. His companions were amused by his serious attention to this and treated it as a joke; but the moment came when The Painter was vindicated. Riled beyond endurance by the Sheikh of the Cataract at Assuan, "he whipped out his pocket-book, ran his finger down the line, and delivered an appropriate quotation. His accent," Amelia Edwards adds, "may not have been faultless; but there could be no mistake as to the energy of his style and the vigour of his language. The effect of both was instantaneous. The Sheykh sprang to his feet as if he had been shot - turned pale with rage under his black skin" and promptly abandoned the boat swearing never to return. (p.198). Consternation ensued but, in fact, the Sheikh was back the next morning, all smiles: "We were his dearest friends now. The Painter was his brother...There was nothing, in short, he would not do to oblige us." After that The Painter's repertory of abuse acquired a different status: "If that note-book of his had been the drowned book of Prospero, or the magical papyrus of Thoth fished up anew from the bottom of the Nile, we could not have regarded it with a respect more nearly bordering upon awe." (p.199)

The tone of amusement is unmistakable in this. The tone of an incident involving The Idle Man is more difficult to determine. Her attitude towards The Idle Man is from the beginning ambiguous. His interest in the Nile journey was for the sake of the shooting rather than the antiquities but at least he earned her approval when he gave up the pursuit of crocodiles on realizing the extent of the slaughter for commercial gain. He continued to shoot birds, however, either for sport or for food. One day he shoots, inadvertently, a native baby. "Hapless Idle Man!" writes Amelia Edwards "- hapless, but homicidal. If he had been content to shoot only quail, and had not taken to shooting babies! What possessed him to do it?" (p.382) The party on the boat heard a woman suddenly scream "a scream with a ring of horror in it" and all at once saw on the bank men and women appearing from nowhere and all running to one spot. Then they saw The Idle Man's native retainer appear, running, and later The Idle Man himself "walking very slowly and defiantly, with his head up, his arms folded, his gun gone, and an immense rabble at his heels" (p.384). It turns out that the baby is only slightly grazed and no serious harm done but what is to be made of Amelia Edwards's tone in her recounting of this affair? The cool irony which works so well in respect of The Painter and his anthology of abuse seems totally misplaced here. The facetious invocation to the "Hapless Idle Man" jars; so does her assent, apparently, to the party's decision that they "felt justified in assuming an injured tone" because, in the first alarm following the shot and the scream, he had been hit on the back of the head with a stone and had his gun wrenched from him. The English agree that the village should be called to account for a "cowardly assault" and immediate restitution of the gun demanded. As a generous concession, they announce that if the gun is returned at once, the father will be permitted to bring the baby on board and it will be attended to: at this stage no one knows the extent of the injuries and, in any event, no one on board has a medical training. The angry crowd is pacified, the baby sponged and plastered and the father given a piece of money. The Painter and The Idle Man then conceive it their duty to take the matter further and "for the protection of future travellers" to lodge a complaint against the village, mainly because of the blow on the head. There follows an experience of the working of the Egyptian judicial system. Fifteen men are chained neck to neck and marched before them, to be disposed of at the Englishmen's pleasure. They insist on the release of all but the guilty one and his sentence they commute to six, rather than one hundred and fifty, strokes of the bastinado. No word of sympathy with the horror of the mother or the terror of the child or the indignation of the crowd appears anywhere in the telling of this story. Only at one point, when the

86

fifteen chained prisoners are brought in, does Amelia Edwards express anything but apparent complacency about English behaviour in the affair. "I am ashamed to write it!" (p.387) she exclaims when the results of her companions' complaint is put before their eyes.

The attitudes and feelings underlying this story are not easily assessed. Most obviously they smack of an imperial arrogance according to which the white man - and specifically the Englishman - and his gun were untouchable and insensitivity to the feelings of lesser breeds was a matter of course. On the other side of the case, the small number of the boat company should be remembered and their extreme vulnerability if the native population turned hostile and felt they could attack with impunity. From this point of view the story may justly celebrate, by implication, their cool-headedness in a seriously threatening situation. The insistence on the proper forms of justice may be said to belong to the best imperial tradition and it is recoil from the abuse of justice which provokes Amelia Edwards to her one direct expression of her reactions. Her apparent indifference to other aspects of the incident, however, is disconcerting. It was never her wont to speak out strongly on matters that might be controversial or delicate. She did not regard herself as a polemicist nor did she think she had a mission to correct or admonish but at least, on this occasion, some expression of sympathy with the natives would have been welcome. Evidently, since the baby was safe, she felt she could afford to treat its grazing lightly and maintain the gently humorous tone of the majority of her anecdotes. By placing her emphasis not on the human drama of distraught mother, angry father and frightened child but on the sense of public duty which impelled the Englishmen to report the village to the local authorities, she avoided the need to disclose any personal feelings, whether of regret, fear, anger or other, which she might have had at the time. The refusal to expose any more than is necessary of intimate personal life is characteristic but in this instance she risks placing herself in an unattractive light.[11]

The same sort of ambiguity in her attitudes is reflected elsewhere. Like Harriet Martineau and Florence Nightingale, Amelia Edwards visited harems and unlike them she also wished to visit a slave-market. She and her companions broached the subject when the black Governor of Assuan and two Arab officials paid a courtesy call on the boat. They soon discovered that they had committed an embarrassing *faux pas* which gravely upset their guests. The Governor and his companions vehemently denied that there was any such market in Assuan. Slave-trading was by this time illegal but the English party had heard on good authority in Cairo that a private bazaar still existed in Assuan. The Governor and his friends would have none of this and could not be persuaded to relax their stance of total probity and scrupulous legality by earnest assurances that the motive of the enquiry was not idle curiosity nor a political axe to grind. "Our only object was sketching", Amelia Edwards writes (p.178), the party's enthusiasm for the visit having been aroused by their Cairo informant who had promised them a particularly fine subject: "of all the sights a traveller might see in Egypt, this was the most curious and pathetic". A few pages later, after an enthusiastic and evocative description of the scenery at the first Cataract, Amelia Edwards herself makes a comment which might well be applied to the slave-market episode. In the beauty and picturesqueness of what is to be seen, she writes, "one is almost in danger of forgetting that the places are something more than beautiful backgrounds, and that the people are not merely appropriate figures placed there for the delight of sketchers, but are made of living flesh and blood, and moved by hopes, and fears, and sorrows, like our own" (p.201). The scene on the boat shows Amelia Edwards once more, as in the baby-wounding, accepting the common attitudes of her time apparently easily and without question[12] but the later comment shows her capable also of a more sensitive awareness. If there were tensions and compromises underlying the persona she constructed for her public rôle, as seems likely, she certainly took care to eliminate all but the slightest traces of an alternative personality.

She visited one harem and L visited others. She found that though the wives of princes and nobles in Cairo and Alexandria had rather more to occupy them, the women of the lesser gentry and upper middle-class were condemned to lives absolutely without mental resources and deprived even of fresh air and exercise. Good-natured and gentle as they were, "their faces bore the expression of people who are habitually bored" (p.480). She concluded that the lives of the peasant women were much superior to those of any other class, in spite of hard work and bitter poverty: "They have the free use of their limbs, and they at least know the fresh air, the sunshine, and the open fields." Her comments are well-judged and sympathetic but at the same time they stand in strong contrast with the chapter on harems in *Eastern Life*. Amelia Edwards did not share Harriet Martineau's passionate commitment to the cause of human dignity and freedom. Her sights were set elsewhere and, though she had a keen sense of women's rights, only one crusade commanded her real dedication. By the time *A Thousand Miles* was published she was quite clear what that crusade was. At the end of the chapter about the new discoveries at Abu Simbel, she speaks out directly and without equivocation. The wall-paintings which had been fresh and beautiful when she and her party uncovered them were, she had been told, already damaged: "Such is the fate of every Egyptian monument, great or small" (p.353). Tourists carve their names and dates all over them and even draw caricatures. Students of Egyptology use harmful processes in their eagerness to take copies. Arabs steal on behalf of collectors who seize voraciously whatever they can get their hands on. "The work of destruction, meanwhile, goes on apace. There is no one to prevent it; there is no one to discourage it". The museums of Europe are rich in plunder wrenched without thought from Egypt and, "When science leads the way, is it wonderful that ignorance should follow?" The task which was to absorb the interests and energies of the rest of her life is set in this paragraph. Governments, national institutions, private individuals must all be brought to understand the value of the remains of the ancient civilization of Egypt and must be urged to exert themselves for their protection. What has already been uncovered must be properly recorded and further excavation must be done on a scientific basis. She came back home to draw up circulars stating the needs and to issue appeals for support. Finally in 1882, by her efforts and with the assistance of R.S. Poole of the British Museum, the Egypt Exploration Fund was established. Under its revised name of The Egypt Exploration Society it continues a very active life today and remembers, as it should, how much it and Egyptology owe to Amelia Edwards.

A Thousand Miles up the Nile marked a turning point in her life. She found her vocation in Egypt as *A Thousand Miles*, with its careful, detailed appreciation of the historic and artistic qualities of the monuments bears witness. She had the advantage over Harriet Martineau that thirty years of research provided her with much more information to work on and she was able to study the sites with better instructed eyes. For contemporaries her book was an excellent guide to what to see and how to see it. *Eastern Life* cannot compete in that respect but, on the other hand, it pulsates with ideas, enthusiasms, repugnancies and by its measure Amelia Edwards's cool ironies and nice judgement of her commitments may seem too bland, too concerned to be acceptable and to avoid offence. That there were other, less mannerly impulses beneath the surface has already been suggested and the treatment of religion in *A Thousand Miles*, muted as it is, offers a final piece of evidence that this was so.

It is a dominant feature of both Harriet Martineau's and Florence Nightingale's accounts of their Nile journeys that they were swept by the impact of Egypt into deep searching of their religious doubts and convictions. The absence of anything like this is equally conspicuous in *A Thousand Miles*. Nevertheless the book is not without clues as to the bent of Amelia Edwards's mind. In her account of the Coptic community which took over the sacred temple of Isis on Philae, her sympathy seems equally divided between the adherents of the old faith and the new. She imagines life in the Christian village which grew up on the island. The village was probably, she thinks, very much like Luxor as it was in her day, noisy with children and dogs "and sleeping at night as soundly as if no ghost-like, mutilated Gods were looking on mournfully in the moonlight" (p.223). If there is some hint of a sense of loss here, there is also some satisfaction that time brings a degree of consolation to the mournful gods: "The Gods are avenged now. The creed which dethroned them is dethroned". Islam is now the dominant faith and only a few ruined convents and a cross or two remain "to show that Christianity once passed that way". Amelia Edwards appears to accept the superseding of one faith by another with as much equanimity as ever Harriet Martineau came to do and whether she herself was deeply committed to any faith is doubtful. *Hand and Glove*, twenty years before, had included an astonishingly violent attack on the works of Christianity and the passing of time had not blunted her capacity for taking a devastatingly unsentimental view of what people can be induced to believe. The Ptolemaic temple at Edfu was, as she notes, built at a time when the ancient Egyptian religion was in decay. Beliefs and practices which had originated in what she calls "a subtle and philosophical core of solar myths" had by then degenerated into mumbo-jumbo. The symbolic meanings of the gods had been forgotten but nevertheless their images were still worshipped with elaborate and costly rituals. "What then of their worshippers?" Amelia Edwards asks. "Did they really believe all these things, or were any of them tormented with doubts of the Gods? Were there sceptics in those days, who wondered how two hierogrammates could look each other in the face without laughing?" (p.405) It seems very likely that she was herself a sceptic of her own day, turning the same challenging and incredulous gaze upon doctrines of the Church of England as she supposes intelligent ancient Egyptians must have directed to those priestly observances still practised long after the true light of their faith had died.

Scepticism is not, however, the whole story. Acerbic as she might be about religion in decay, she was not, on occasion at least, insensible of the pull of a mysterious and non-rational world or immune to its influence. An experience at Abu Simbel shows her for once reacting to "the mystic and magical" qualities of Egypt, her interest in which impressed Wallis Budge. Abu Simbel acted strongly upon Amelia Edwards as it had on Harriet Martineau and Florence Nightingale before her. She spent fourteen days there and every morning of the fourteen she watched the effect of the first light of dawn on the figures of Rameses II on the façade of the Great Temple. For one moment in that light they seemed to come to conscious life: "I brought myself almost to believe at last that there must sooner or later come some one sunrise when the ancient charm would snap asunder, and the giants must arise and speak" (p.285). She liked to be alone in the temple where, deep inside the rock, "The very Gods assert their ancient influence over those who question them in solitude...There were times when I felt I believed in them" (p.304). Yet there was something about the place which she found "weird and awful" and she shrank from going alone into the far interior. On one occasion, however, she ventured to the furthest recess and sat at the feet of the gods in the sanctuary. Then, quite unexpectedly, she was seized by panic. It flashed into her mind that the whole weight of the mountain into which the temple was cut hung over her head and might collapse on her. She tried to run and, as in a nightmare, felt she could not and that she had no voice to call for help. "It is unnecessary, perhaps", she goes on in her more usual cool way, "to add that the mountain did not cave in, and that I had my fright for nothing. It would have been a grand way of dying all the same; and a still grander way of being buried" (p.305).

This is a striking episode. Abu Simbel is still a place of extraordinary power but the modern visitor does not see it as nineteenth century travellers did. A visit then was inevitably different in kind from what it is now. To their eyes paintings and reliefs emerged mysteriously by the light of candles and flares and the statues of the gods in the inner sanctuary did not sit all day under electric light, as now they do, but came suddenly out of the darkness from the depths of the original mountain.[13] Harriet Martineau found there reinforcement of her respect for the ancient gods and Florence Nightingale was overwhelmed by the grandeur of the ideas she felt that it embodied. Like Amelia Edwards, both were able to visit it alone and feel the full force of its symbols and its ancient silence. Only in Amelia Edwards did the experience produce terror and it seems unlikely that a sudden spasm of claustrophobia, in evidence nowhere else, was entirely responsible for it. Here, more dramatically than elsewhere, is evidence of the existence in Amelia Edwards of aspects of mind and feeling which she kept, for most of the time, carefully submerged in the interests of a career which depended always on the favour of the public, whether the stakes were her own livelihood or the functioning of the Egypt Exploration Fund. Her views about religion, about the position of women, about the behaviour of her countrymen, she suppressed except for the occasional glimpse which could be easily passed over. The potency of the old gods, however, in the quiet and the darkness broke her control for one remarkable moment and confronted her with forces within herself with which she had played in her stories of the supernatural but which now terrified her when they threatened to break into the carefully controlled persona she had constructed. She fled into the daylight and, as she presents the story in *A Thousand Miles*, tossed the whole episode off with a resumption of her usual ironic composure. That so disciplined a woman should have been so profoundly affected is one of the most impressive demonstrations of the forceful impact which the ideas and images of ancient Egypt could make.

In their writings about Egypt Harriet Martineau and Florence Nightingale contribute directly or indirectly to knowledge and understanding of some of the most crucial issues of nineteenth century debate, about religion, about the destiny of man, about the position of women. Amelia Edwards does not deal explicitly with such matters. The big idea which comes to fill her life and by which she makes her major contribution to the intellectual and artistic life of her century and beyond, is her passionate dedication to the saving and studying of the monuments of ancient Egypt. She was herself only an amateur scholar but as one of the prime movers in the development of Egyptology in this country her achievement stands without parallel. *A Thousand Miles up the Nile* is part of that achievement in that it stimulated interest and popularized the subject without demeaning it - as it continues to do. It is also a highly accomplished piece of writing by a writer of considerable gifts and it brings into prominence a woman whose personality fascinates while at the same time it baffles investigation. Attempts to fill in the meagre biographical facts available have so far met with little success but a full life of Amelia Edwards, if it can be written, would be a valuable addition to the history of nineteenth century women.[14]

For Harriet Martineau, Florence Nightingale and Amelia Edwards, a visit to Egypt was a precipitating agent, throwing into new patterns their thoughts and, for two of them at least, their lives. It acted in each case upon women constrained by conventions which denied or at best obstructed their full self-development. Ancient Egypt gave them another world, set in wider perspective and governed by different assumptions about life and death. It gave them gods who were benign, far unlike the stern patriarch of Victorian churches, and goddesses who were beautiful givers of life and love. It stimulated their minds and imaginations with a history, an art and a landscape not yet dominated by professional authority and on which they could exercise their own powers of interpretation and discrimination. Unlike the classical world, pored over for hundreds of years by schoolboys and scholars, ancient Egypt offered a relatively uncharted field in which a woman might make a substantial and original contribution to knowledge and understanding. For all these reasons, Egypt had a special meaning and appeal for women equipped by nature and education to respond to it. The visit to Egypt was an intellectual and spiritual event in Harriet Martineau's life, a spiritual one in Florence Nightingale's and primarily, it would seem, a psychological one in Amelia Edwards's for it gave a centre to her existence in which all the elements of her nature could be absorbed, or if not absorbed, pacified. Egypt did not mean the same or so much to the men who came but for these women it was a crucial experience. Their records, each in its way brilliantly composed, are rich in content and in character. They can be read in many ways - casually, for the entertainment they offer; as research material for many kinds of enquiry; as contributions to the biographies of three exceptionally interesting women; but in their totality they are not easily exhaustible. As Egypt made an impact upon them, so they, in their response to Egypt, make an impact on readers today.

Chapter IV

"When one sits among the people"

The Egypt which made so forceful an impact on Harriet Martineau, Florence Nightingale and Amelia Edwards was predominantly ancient Egypt. They did not ignore the present, Harriet Martineau in particular, with her usual keen interest in social questions, taking some pains to enquire into the condition of the people. With the time at her disposal she could get no more, as she frankly acknowledged, than an outsider's view and her chapter on the "present condition of Egypt" is cautious though perceptive. Florence Nightingale and Amelia Edwards were aware, as they could hardly fail to be, of the miserable state of the people and the abuse of privilege and authority at all levels of society. Florence Nightingale recoiled in disgust at what she saw. Amelia Edwards grieved but felt helpless and made a point, after early experiences, of avoiding the native towns so that she might escape the sight of their poverty, sickness and squalor. The condition of the children, especially, she found so distressing "that one would willingly go any number of miles out of the way rather than witness their suffering, without the power to alleviate it".[1] All three of them were, essentially, visitors to Egypt, travelling there to share in the great discoveries of the ancient past which excited the intellectual world and it is entirely understandable that, with their minds fixed on other objectives, they averted their eyes as far as they could from problems they had no power to solve.

Another woman, their contemporary, with different reasons for being in Egypt, saw it and wrote about it from a different point of view. Her experience gives another dimension to this story of nineteenth century women's encounter with Egypt. What she has to say does not invalidate the accounts which have been discussed in previous chapters but it enlarges the context in which they were set. Her angle of vision brings into prominence what is only background in them, for she focuses on the actualities of contemporary Egypt and its native inhabitants. These were subjects not readily visible from the dahabiehs and steamers which plied up and down the Nile with their cargoes of well-heeled Europeans bent on replenishing the intellectual stores of the western world.

"Mr Arrowsmith kindly gave me Miss Martineau's book which I have begun. It is true as far as it goes, but there is the usual defect - the people are not real people, only part of the scenery to her, as to most Europeans." So wrote Lucie Duff Gordon in a letter of January 20, 1864. Lady Duff Gordon and Harriet Martineau were distant cousins but their experience of Egypt followed a quite different path, as did the rest of their lives. Born in 1821 and therefore much the same age as Florence Nightingale, Lucie Duff Gordon began to develop tuberculosis in the 1850s. She was married and by 1858 had three children but in search of health she went, alone, first to South Africa and then, in 1862, to Egypt. For the rest of her life she lived mainly in Luxor with occasional visits to Cairo where her husband met her in 1864 and to Alexandria where her married daughter, Janet Ross, lived. She paid one visit to England in 1863. The letters she wrote home to her husband, her mother and her daughter were published and went through several editions.[2] Egypt's climate delayed the development of her illness but could not finally halt it and she died in Cairo in 1869. Nevertheless, the growing popularity of Egypt as a health resort during the latter part of the century evidently owed something to her example. There is some irony in this for Lucie Duff Gordon and her seven years in Egypt were in every way exceptional. It was the longest period any European had spent in Upper Egypt but, more than that, the way in which she lived and what she made of her circumstances were quite unique.

The house she occupied in Luxor had been built about 1815 over the sanctuary of the temple by Henry Salt, then English Consul-General in Egypt. Belzoni live there for a time in his employ but later the house became the property of the French Government and was known as The French House. Champollion stayed there while he was working in the area in 1829 and so did the French officers sent out in 1831 to remove one of the two obelisks which stood in front of the pylons and transport it to Paris. (The obelisk now stands in the Place de la Concorde.) Lady

Duff Gordon acquired the use of the house in December 1863 and arrived there from Cairo a month later. "My palace" she calls it, "such a big rambling house." It was very dirty with the dust of three unoccupied years, but "my room looks quite handsome with carpets and a divan" (p.101). The staircase had fallen in but was soon repaired. Two owls and a hawk became familiar but a snake had to be killed. (Snakes and scorpions were to become more troublesome later.) The letters offer very little further description of the house, either at this point or in subsequent years, but Amelia Edwards saw it four years after Lady Duff Gordon's death. She sketched it and in *A Thousand Miles up the Nile* described it and also its surroundings. The house itself, "an old tumble-down building...a rude structure of palm-timbers and sun-dried clay"[3] had deteriorated, like her health, while Lucie Duff Gordon still lived in it. Part of it had collapsed but the rooms she had last inhabited could still be visited in 1873: "Her couch, her rug, her folding chair were there still. The walls were furnished with a few cheap prints and a pair of tin sconces. All was very bare and comfortless...We were shocked at the dreariness of the place."[4] The view, however, overlooking the Nile and the western plain of Thebes, was magnificent. It "furnished the room and made its poverty splendid". Lucie Duff Gordon had herself exclaimed about the view when she first saw the house but she had not described what was less magnificent in the scene around her. The obelisks, colossi and the entrance pylon were buried to a depth of forty feet while the interior of the temple had over the centuries become the site of an Arab village. Hundreds of years of village life had raised the floor fifty feet above the original pavement and over the buried remains there stood, until the 1880s when the temple was finally cleared, two large mansions, the French House, some thirty mud huts and eighty straw sheds, together with yards, stables and pigeon-towers.[5] Beyond the entrance, as Amelia Edwards describes it in *A Thousand Miles*, "lay a smoky, filthy, intricate labyrinth of lanes and passages...buffaloes, camels, donkeys, dogs, and human beings were seen herding together in unsavoury fellowship. Cocks crew, hens cackled, pigeons cooed, turkeys gobbled, children swarmed, women were baking and gossiping, and all the sordid routine of Arab life was going on, amid winding alleys that masked the colonnades and defaced the inscriptions of the Pharaohs".[6] Florence Nightingale in 1849 was revolted by what she saw: "The contrast could not be more terrible than the savages of the Present in the temples of the Past at Luxor."[7] Harriet Martineau was similarly shocked by the contrast of past and present and by the sight of the "apish creatures" who now populated the plain of Thebes, once the heart of an advanced civilization and a sophisticated culture.

For Lucie Duff Gordon there was no question of "the sordid routine of Arab life" and the defacement of Pharaonic inscriptions did not greatly concern her. The monuments of the past which seized so strongly on the imaginations of Harriet Martineau, Florence Nightingale and Amelia Edwards moved her too, especially Philae, but everything that could be said about them had been said, she thought, and to add more would be a waste of time. She found her stimulus to mental and moral activity elsewhere and relics of the past, however fine, gripped her attention much less than the men, women and children of the present whom she saw, not as savages, but as individuals to whom was owing the same kind of consideration and respect as to any others. *Eastern Life*, she wrote, contains excellent descriptions but Harriet Martineau "evidently knew and cared nothing about the people, and had the feeling of most English people here, that the difference of manners is a sort of impassable gulf, the truth being that their feelings and passions are just like our own." (pp.111-12). Her comment is unfair to Harriet Martineau but from Lucie Duff Gordon's perspective no English or other traveller, sailing in their comfortable boats with their attentive native crews and venturing on shore only in the company of escorts, often armed, could have any but the most superficial knowledge of the Egyptian people and their way of life. Looking at the vivid paintings and sculptures of nobles and fellahs long dead and gone, most could be stirred and perhaps shaken by recognition that here were men and women who had lived and loved and rejoiced and suffered three thousand years ago in ways still intimately familiar to the well-to-do Europeans who gazed at them from such a different background of time and place. It was much more difficult for these same Europeans to recognize fellow-feeling in the ragged creatures they saw at work in the fields or encountered in the villages, who lived in close proximity to animals and ate with their fingers and were uncompromisingly alien.

Harriet Martineau's own deepest thoughts and impulses were stirred by ancient Egypt and she went on to use what she found there to stir her compatriots similarly and rouse them to a wider view of life and what she saw as humanity's place in the totality of things. Ancient Egypt crystallized things deep in Florence Nightingale also and the experience contributed to the momentum which powered her later life. Amelia Edwards, coming to Egypt with her own history and background, found there a focus for all her energies as she laboured to stimulate care and understanding of the ancient past. For each in her way Egypt was a call to a campaign for greater enlightenment. It was this also for Lucie Duff Gordon but her cause was different from that of any of the others. Her sights were set, not on the past nor on the interests and activities of another country, but on those figures in a landscape whom it was so easy to see merely as good sketching material or, at closer quarters, as degraded beings to be controlled and kept at bay by cudgellings, whippings and abuse. In the ragged uncouth dwellers in the hovels of Luxor she found men, and occasionally women, of dignity, grace and natural courtesy. She found among her neighbours intelligence and sometimes learning. She found compassion and generosity and unselfishness. She dined happily in mud houses devoid of furniture and with the very minimum of equipment: "One learns to think it quite natural to sit with perfect gentlemen in places inferior to our cattle-sheds", she writes (p.110) and she ate unhesitatingly and with relish dishes cooked, served and shared by brown and black fingers. She did not waver in her Christianity but she gladly attended Muslim services and festivals when invited and never failed in respect, not through any effort but through sympathy. She sat with the sick and tended them as best she could. Occasionally she acknowledges that back at home her behaviour would be considered not merely eccentric but reprehensible. One young man whom she was called to see was very ill: "There he lay in a dark little den with bare mud walls, worse off to our ideas, than any pauper." (p.110) She put her arm round him to support him and he held up his face, like a child, for a kiss. "I suppose if I confessed to kissing a 'dirty Arab' in a 'hovel'," she writes, pointedly using the language of her fellow-countrymen, "the English travellers would execrate me." The thought is of little interest to her and she takes occasion to comment instead on the way in which the family, very pious Muslims, respond to her kindness with gratitude and blessings, not at all with the bigotry and fanaticism which according to accepted English wisdom made them implacably hostile to all Christians.

To open the hearts and minds of a northern people, proud of their achievements and power, to a southern race subjected for hundreds of years to foreign domination, deficient in the disciplines and manners of status and authority, was perhaps a harder task even than to persuade them that some intellectual areas still remained outside the reach of their colonization; but in the last analysis the disparate efforts of Harriet Martineau, Florence Nightingale, Amelia Edwards and Lucie Duff Gordon all tended in the same direction - to expand the intellectual and emotional world of an imperial power whose territorial dominions stretched wider still and wider but whose powers of imaginative understanding were less elastic. Lucie Duff Gordon claimed only to deal with people, not with ideas, but to deal with the poor and despised of Egypt as sentient beings sharing a common humanity was, in fact, to unleash a very big idea. She rejected all blanket categories of white, black or brown and wrote, very remarkably for her day and not superfluously more than a hundred years later: "I myself have seen at least five sorts of blacks (Negroes, not Arabs) more unlike each other than Swedes are unlike Spaniards; and many are just like ourselves...I am fully convinced that custom and education are the only real differences between one set of men and another, their inner nature is the same all the world over." (p.307)

What she did is too admirable to be sentimentalized and it is only right and proper to acknowledge that there were, as there were bound to be, limits to the extent of her acceptance of and within Arab society. As a European she commanded automatic respect and as an educated woman, willing and even eager to talk to the better informed and thoughtful among the local men, she received special homage and devotion. She moved, as she said, among "the county families" of Luxor and its environs, consorted with "respectable people" and "high-bred", cultivated Arabs, though she was far from ignoring or neglecting the lowlier inhabitants, the donkey boys, the water carriers or the little children seated in the courtyard round the mosque receiving their lessons from the Koran. She was, inevitably, in a privileged position and, though she used her influence for good whenever and however she could, the barrier of education and background between her and those she lived among could never entirely be wished away. Sometimes she wondered if she really did *quite* understand them and knew that they could never quite understand her. She was much annoyed by Harriet Martineau's account of harems and by her attack on polygamy, arguing that polygamy was sometimes a mark of unselfishness rather than sensual indulgence, as when a man would accept responsibility for his deceased brother's wife and children in order to protect them, though at a cost to himself. She makes the fair point that Harriet Martineau's experience of harems (like those of Florence Nightingale and Amelia Edwards) was among the rich and argues that the justified abomination they aroused should not count as a slur on all Egyptians. The multiple households of the poor might be caring places, offering some shelter from the pressures of a hard life. Her view is a useful reminder of aspects of Egypt that Harriet Martineau, Florence Nightingale and Amelia Edwards did not see but it is also in its way a partial one. She depicts the men as caring towards their women folk and does not enquire far into the lives and feelings of the women themselves. She had, of course, far more in common with the men whose freedom of movement and social intercourse she shared. The women, by their lack of education and the nature of their lives, were largely beyond her reach. It was not her business, as she construed it, to take arms against the prevailing social institutions, whether polygamy, child marriage or slavery, any more than it was to attempt to convert God-fearing Muslims to Christianity. Errors and imperfections were easy to see: the need, as she understood it, was to stress positive qualities and active virtues in order to combat the prejudice and ignorance of those who could recognize little to respect but much to deride and abominate. Like Harriet Martineau who tried always to stretch her mind to empathize with the motivations which created and sustained social customs - even South Sea Island cannibalism - totally unacceptable as on the surface they might be, Lucie Duff Gordon also sought to enter into unfamiliar ways of thought and feeling. Harriet Martineau's standards were passionately intellectual and not to be compromised. Lucie Duff Gordon, less dedicated to ideas, put her emphasis instead, in the matter of polygamy as in others, on the human need for loving-kindness and for relief from illness and poverty and injustice. There are limitations and dangers in both these approaches as there are also values and virtues. Harriet Martineau was more earnestly concerned with contemporary Egypt than either Florence Nightingale or Amelia Edwards. Lucie Duff Gordon was more intimately knowledgeable about the life of the people than any of them. Her commentary and Harriet Martineau's complement and correct each other and both redound greatly to the credit of these women of courage and character who engaged all their energies in the causes they championed.

The political situation in Egypt deteriorated disastrously while Lucie Duff Gordon lived there and the terrible distress of the rural population becomes an increasingly dominant theme in her letters. The European powers admired Ismail Pasha's zeal for westernization but the need for money to carry out their ruler's schemes imposed a fearsome squeeze upon the people. Lucie Duff Gordon saw at first hand the sufferings which resulted. Exorbitant taxation, seizure of goods and forced labour, accompanied by imprisonment, beatings and atrocities reduced people she knew as friends to the direst misery and starvation. The Egyptian government had seemed bad enough to Harriet Martineau at an earlier period and Florence Nightingale had been utterly alienated by what she saw of its practices: "Let no one live in the East, who can find a corner in the ugliest, coldest hole in Europe", she wrote.[8] Amelia Edwards saw something of the harsh effects of forced labour under Ismail's regime but this, like other causes, she acknowledged but did not feel called to fight for. Harsh as it was, it was probably, she thought, a necessary evil.[9] Only Lucie Duff Gordon felt the miseries of the poor as in her own person: "one's pity becomes a perfect passion, when one *sits among the people* as I do, and sees it all", she writes (p.240) and she forecasts trouble to come.

She was right in this. By 1875 the country was bankrupt and Egyptian nationalism was on the rise. To protect its own interests Britain occupied Egypt in 1882 and a long period of tutelage and trouble began. Numbered among those who administered Egypt during these years of what was effectively British rule was Lord Edward Cecil. When he died in 1918 he had served for fifteen years in various capacities, latterly as Financial Adviser to the Egyptian Government. His role, by his own account, was in effect to ensure that a degree of order was achieved in a situation bedevilled by incompetence or greed or both. His sketches of life in Cairo[10] are highly entertaining but the picture which emerges of a country debased in the recent past by the abuses of its Turkish-sponsored governors and later humiliated by foreign occupation and domination is in itself a shameful one. That things should have come to this would have been no surprise to Lucie Duff Gordon, Harriet Martineau would have drawn many lessons from it, Florence Nightingale and Amelia Edwards would probably have been content that British administration was at any rate greatly superior to anything on offer before 1882. All of them would have been able to savour fully the fact that when, in June 1956, General abd al-Nasser became President, Egypt was ruled by an Egyptian for the first time since the Thirtieth Dynasty of the fourth century B.C.

Napoleon's invasion of 1798 gave a stimulus to Egyptological study which has not yet been exhausted and incidentally opened the door for tourism and for the impact of west upon east which inevitably followed. Since then Egypt has drastically changed. Not only has the structure of government been transformed but the building of the High Dam has altered the topography, even to some extent the climate, of a country which for centuries, even millennia, had followed the same pattern of life. Changes were already beginning when Harriet Martineau, Florence Nightingale and Amelia Edwards travelled there, their presence being itself a feature of change though none could have known then how inexorable processes, once initiated, would develop. Altered as Egypt is, however, its potent attraction remains and the nature of that attraction stays constant. Those who know little about Egyptian politics and care as little about the workers in the fields or the figures glimpsed in towns and villages, travel in their thousands to see the sights of the Nile. How great or small the impact Egypt makes depends, as ever, on the receiving mind. That it can be as considerable today as in the past has been demonstrated by the examples quoted in the first chapter. The particular mix of ideas and temperamental urges which stirred Harriet Martineau, Florence Nightingale and Amelia Edwards is unlikely to be duplicated for it belonged to a specific period in British history. The record of the effect of Egypt on minds and personalities so conditioned retains, however, its power to fascinate and to stimulate.

Lucie Duff Gordon brings to life the contemporary realities which others passed by in their pursuit of the Pharaonic grandeurs of the past. Her warm and vivid writing delights and entertains;[11] it also pricks the conscience about all undervalued and neglected peoples at home and abroad. The abuse of greatness, however, is always with us, like the poor and all their attendant social problems. Such matters constitute the business of every generation and are the pressing concerns of every day. Ancient Egypt, on the other hand, lifts the mind beyond today and tomorrow and invites contemplation of the dimensions of history and the experience of fellow beings in far-off recesses of time. Scientists find ripples deep in space which speak to them of the earliest moments of the creation of matter. Their discovery excites the intelligence but it gives human sympathy little to feed on. The relics of ancient Egypt, by contrast, give an intimate picture of the earliest history of humanity as we know it. The dwellers in the towns and temples, villages and palaces two or three thousand years before the Christian era were men and women in all ways very much like ourselves - not anthropoids emerging from primeval forests or uncouth savages pursuing a primitive existence. Their memorials and the personal records which survive are those of cultivated and learned individuals living within a sophisticated society, one, which at its best was animated by a highly developed system of thought. Nowhere else is it possible to know so much from firsthand evidence about so long ago. The encounter of citizens of modern states with dwellers by the Nile four thousand years ago excites awe and respect and also the fear which is born of the mystery of time; Harriet Martineau, Florence Nightingale and

Amelia Edwards responded with all the force of their natures to the stimulus of the experience. Ancient Egypt put questions to them as it continues to do to today's travellers and they sought the answers vigorously and whole-heartedly. They did not have the knowledge of modern Egyptologists but their deficiencies in this regard are of little significance: their accounts of Egypt rest on deep foundations and they stand the test of time.

Notes

Introduction

1.   See John Pemble, *The Mediterranean Passion*, Clarendon Press, Oxford, 1987, pp.68-9.
2.   Florence Nightingale's *Letters from Egypt*, ed. Anthony Sattin, Barrie and Jenkins, London, 1987, p.217.
3.   An interesting list is offered by Harriet Martineau in Appendix B to *Eastern Life Present and Past* (Moxon, London, 1848), together with much practical advice.
4.   Kate Bradbury, for some time companion-secretary to Amelia Edwards, came from Ashton. She married Francis Griffith who began his career as an assistant to Flinders Petrie and later succeeded him as Professor of Archaeology at London. I am indebted to my neighbour, Mr A.S. Ashton for drawing my attention to Haslam Mills's book and for his notes on it.
5.   *Eothen*, Macmillan, London, 1935, p.xix. All quotations are from this edition.
6.   For example, see "The Hareem" from Richard Monckton Milnes's collection *Palm Leaves*:

> The deep affections of the West
> With thought of life's sublimest ends
> Ne'er to the Eastern home deny
> Its lesser, yet not humble praise,
> To guard one pure humanity
> Amid the stains of evil days

7.   Vivant Denon, a leading scholar in Napoleon's train of *savants*, gives striking testimony to the impact of a first sight of Thebes. "As the ancient city first came into view," he writes, "the whole [French] army, suddenly and with one accord, stood in amazement at the sight of its scattered ruins, and clapped their hands with delight". Peter Clayton, *The Rediscovery of Ancient Egypt*, (Thames and Hudson, London, 1982, repr. 1990, p.103). Denon himself made invaluable drawings and descriptions of the sites as they were at the end of the eighteenth century.
8.   Edward Lear, *Selected Letters*, ed. Vivien Noakes, Clarendon Press, Oxford, 1988, p.127.
9.   *Further Recollections of a Happy Life*, Macmillan, London, 1893, pp.119-20. There are ebullient letters from Marianne North to Amelia Edwards ("my dearest Amy") in the library of Somerville College, Oxford.

10. The squeaking and groaning of the sakia, a primitive device for raising water, was a torment to the western ear but Harriet Martineau had the imagination to understand that to the Nile peasant the same noise made "the sweetest and most heart-stirring music in the world", telling of "provision, property, wonted occupation, home, the beautiful Nile, and beloved oxen" (*Eastern Life,* p.137). Not many travellers on the Nile were capable of such empathy.
11. D.G. Rossetti, "The Burden of Nineveh".
12. Published Faber, London, 1971.
13. Egyptologists have named a predynastic ruler King Scorpion after the ideogram on a monumental mace. Golding has evidently been attracted by the emblematic qualities of the name.
14. Published by Hodder and Stoughton, London, Sydney, Auckland, Toronto, 1989.
15. The words are quoted by Harriet Martineau, with approval, from a book by the Hon. Charles Leonard Irby and James Mangles, *Travels in Egypt, Nubia, Syria and Asia Minor during the years 1817 and 1818* (Darf Publishers Ltd., London, 1895). Irby and Mangles, both Commanders in the Royal Navy, had many difficulties in their travels both with terrain and natives but their account is admirably straightforward and good-tempered. They were with Belzoni when he opened the temple at Abu Simbel in August 1817 and were among the handful of Europeans who, together with a Turkish soldier, worked for ten hours a day for seventeen days clearing away the sand, the natives having withdrawn their labour.
16. Florence Nightingale, *Letters from Egypt*, p.77.

Chapter I

1. *Harriet Martineau's Autobiography*, i, p.402. The autobiography was first published in 1877. All quotations in this book are from the Virago edition, 1983.
2. *Autobiography*, i. p.133.
3. Quoted in *Harriet Martineau* by Valerie Pichanick (University of Michigan Press, 1980), p.239.
4. *Deerbrook* was published by Virago in 1983 but is unfortunately again out of print.
5. *Autobiography*, ii, p.345.
6. *Eastern Life Present and Past*, p.321. All references are to the 1880 edition. The book was first published by Moxon in 1848.
7. "Rose-red city" is Burgon's but the phrase "half as old as time" had earlier appeared in Samuel Rogers's poem "Italy" of 1822.
8. *Letters on the Laws of Man's Nature and Development* consists of an exchange of letters between Harriet Martineau and George Henry Atkinson, a man with pretensions to science. He was a mesmerist and

when she first met him Harriet Martineau had already submitted herself to mesmerism and believed that it had cured her of her illness. He was also a phrenologist and under his influence she became increasingly interested in phrenology, seeing it as an advance towards the scientific understanding of processes of mind. Unfortunately she greatly over-estimated Atkinson's sagacity and abilities and her association with him encouraged her to develop her ideas to insupportable lengths with results which gravely damaged her reputation as a serious thinker.

For a discussion of the *Letters* and their reception, see Pichanick, pp.182-92. Fuller accounts than are relevant here of the background and development of Harriet Martineau's ideas are to be found in Pichanick's excellent study.

9. Quoted Pichanick, p.191.
10. Harriet Martineau's habit of introducing, without warning, far-fetched references in unexpected contexts (as in comparing entering Petra to being drawn up out of a coal pit) may put a strain on the reader's gravity. Explaining the value of being prepared to enter open-mindedly into alien ideas and practices, she writes earnestly: "I vividly remember the satisfaction of ascertaining the ideas that lay at the bottom of those most barbarous South Sea island practices of Human Sacrifice and Cannibalism"! p.110.
11. Harriet Martineau's information about brothels may derive from Florence Nightingale with whom she corresponded for many years. Florence Nightingale's experiences in the Crimea gave her ample opportunity to become acquainted with the life of prostitutes as with all other aspects of army life. She campaigned strongly against the introduction of the Contagious Diseases Act of 1864 which gave police in garrison towns and ports the right to arrest, detain and examine any woman suspected of being a prostitute. Rather than persecuting women she argued, effort should be directed to attacking the conditions which encouraged prostitution. She asked for Harriet Martineau's support, which was readily given, and supplied figures for a series of articles Harriet Martineau wrote for *The Daily News*.
12. Harriet Martineau was among those who supported and signed the first petition for women's suffrage in 1866.

Chapter II

1. *Letters from Egypt: a Journey on the Nile*, selected and introduced by Anthony Sattin, Barrie and Jenkins, London, 1987. All quotations, except where otherwise indicated, are from this edition. A full edition of the letters was privately printed by Florence Nightingale's sister in 1854. The material omitted by the recent editor does not substantially affect the content and style of the letters as presented.

2.   These notes are printed in *Florence Nightingale, 1820-1910*, by Cecil Woodham-Smith, (Constable, London, 1950), p.17. The original *carnet de poche* which Florence Nightingale used in Egypt is in the British Library, B.M. Add. Mss. 45,846.

3.   *The Cause*, London, G. Bell and Sons, 1928. "Cassandra" has recently been reprinted by Pickering and Chatto (1991).

4.   See, for example, her contempt for the painted tombs of Eilethyia (modern El Kab). Only one thing recommended them: "There is one comfort...to be drawn from them, that the conventionalities of social life are the same in the two ends of Time and Space - the master and the mistress sitting before dinner, with the company in rows, the ladies smelling at their nosegays, and a little music to amuse them, is exactly what 100 mistresses of 100 country houses endure every day in an island the Egyptians never heard of, and at a time 4000 years off", p.123. Harriet Martineau responded to the tombs in a very different spirit, rejoicing in the view they gave of the everyday life of ordinary people - "how far back in the depths of time!" - but she had never had to "endure" - the word expresses everything - a remorseless social life which was at the same time exhausting and pointless.

5.   The full title of this book, which was never published, was *Suggestions for Thought to Searchers after Truth among the Artizans of England*. The B.L. copy has manuscript annotations by John Stuart Mill.

6.   *Eastern Life Present and Past*, p.62.

7.   *Eastern Life*, p.63.

8.   *Eastern Life*, pp.41 and 43.

9.   B.M. Add. Mss. 45,847.

10.   See *Eastern Life*, pp.7 and 42-3. Flaubert, who was travelling in Egypt at the same time as Florence Nightingale, was struck by the architectural quality of everything in Egypt. The palm, he wrote, is "an architectural tree": "Everything in Egypt seems made for architecture - the planes of the field, the vegetation, the human anatomy, the horizon lines". (*Flaubert in Egypt*, ed. Francis Steegmuller, Bodley Head, London, Sydney, Toronto, 1972, p.58.)

11.   Harriet Martineau notes that in early Egyptian thinking "good and evil were supposed to be nearly related, and both claiming homage, as necessary and therefore worthy of acceptance" (*Eastern Life*, p.151), but she does not develop this. The idea does not mesh in with her thought and experience.

        The modern couple at the centre of John Fowles's *Daniel Martin* find, like Florence Nightingale, that an ancient relief speaks directly to them (pp.532-33).

12.   *The Life of Florence Nightingale* by Sir Edward Cook, 2 vols., London, Macmillan, 1913, i, p.469.

13.   See note 5.

14.   *Letters from Egypt*, Eyre and Spottiswood, London, 1864 (privately printed), pp.139-40.

15. Shelley's famous poem, "Ozymandias", written in 1817, is on the same theme. Shelley, who did not visit Egypt, was misinformed about the characteristic expression given to Rameses II (Ozymandias) on his statues.

16. "An Egyptian novel", she wrote earlier, "apparently begins with a man's death" (p.40).

17. The aquatic monks were a notorious feature of the journey. Flaubert found the episode amusing: "It was a *tutti* of cudgelings, pricks, bare arses, yells and laughter" (*Flaubert in Egypt*, p.127).

18. Woodham-Smith, *Florence Nightingale*, p.107.

19. Idem., p.128.

20. Some comments of Anthony Trollope in his novel *The Bertrams*, (1859) seem not inappropriate to the mosque episode. "None but Englishmen or English women", he writes, "do such things as this. To other people is wanting sufficient pluck for such enterprises, is wanting also a certain mixture of fun, honest independence, and bad taste." (Chap. IX)

Florence Nightingale scores over Trollope, however, in her account of the pyramids. At least she gets some comedy out of her visit to the interior whereas he is merely bad-tempered: "nothing is to be gained by entering the pyramid except dirt, noise, stench, vermin, abuse, and want of air. (*The Bertrams*, chap. XXXVIII)

21. Woodham-Smith, *Florence Nightingale*, p.128.

Chapter III

1. Published by Century, London, Sydney, Auckland, Johannesburg, 1984. Page references are to the 1989 reissue. The book was reprinted by Parkway (paperback) and Darf (hardback) in 1993.

2. An article by her cousin, Matilda Betham Edwards (1836-1919), is a prime source of what information there is about Amelia Edwards's background and early life. It was published in *The New England Magazine* for January, 1893. Miss Betham Edwards was herself a prolific writer of, among other things, novels and travel books and readers were liable to confuse the work of the two cousins.

3. There is a reference to MacCready on p.157 of *A Thousand Miles* suggesting that Amelia Edwards herself was well acquainted with his style of acting if not with him.

4. See especially "My Home Life", published in *Arena*, 1891, pp.299-310.

5. Sir E.A. Wallis Budge, *By Nile and Tigris*, (Murray, London, 1920), i, p.101, note 1. The obituarist in *The Saturday Review* of April 23, 1892, makes a similar point about her tact and disinterestedness: "Living in the midst of controversies, she always kept herself aloof. The sweet-

ness of her temper in this respect set an example to many who intellectually were her superiors".

6. The American lectures were afterwards published by Osgood, Mellvaine and Co., London, 1891, under the title *Pharaohs, Fellahs and Explorers*. (The title was not her choice.)

7. Quoted from the Petrie Papers by Margaret S. Drower in *Flinders Petrie*, (London, 1985), p.199.

8. "The Queen of Egyptology" by William Copley Winslow in *The American Antiquarian*, XIV, no.6, Nov. 1892, pp.305-15. W.C. Winslow, Honorary Secretary of the Egypt Exploration Fund for the United States, was a devoted admirer of Amelia Edwards. "She knew the *whole* field of Egyptology," he writes, "better than any man, and no one could approach her word power to describe the field, on the side of history, art and exploration." He notes, however, that "Miss Edwards's genius belongs to the objective rather than the subjective school; and she assiduously cultivated her powers and tastes in the direction of objects rather than subjects of thought, or, if the latter, from without rather than from within." His remark raises, but does not settle, a recurrent question in the study of Amelia Edwards: did she not have a "subjective" life or did she choose to suppress it?

9. Budge, op.cit., p.101, note 1.

10. For other examples see the bazaar at Minieh (p.83) and a bird-life idyll at Abydos (p.470).

11. The dahabieh in which Amelia Edwards travelled, called The Philae, was accompanied much of the time by The Bagstones, carrying Miss Marianne Brocklehurst of Macclesfield and her party. There was a good deal of friendly communication between the groups and among other references to "the M.B's" are several to Alfred, Miss Brocklehurst's nephew, "a man of pronounced sporting tastes". "On 2nd March [1873]", Miss Brocklehurst notes in her diary, "Alfred went shooting and peppered a native by mistake" *Macclesfield Collection of Egyptian Antiquities* by Rosalie David (Aris and Phillips Ltd, Warminster, 1980, p.11). In *sang froid* this rivals Amelia Edwards. Perhaps "peppering natives" was too common an occurrence to be fussed over?

12. The Brocklehurst group negotiated for an Abyssinian slave girl in Nubia. The deal fell through for reasons Amelia Edwards does not make clear. She makes no comment on the attempted transaction and her description of the girl as "this useful article" could be taken as her readers wished (pp.356-7).

13. Both temples at Abu Simbel have been resited to raise them above the waters of Lake Nasser. This remarkable feat of engineering was completed in 1969.

14. A biography is in course of preparation by Miss Brenda Moon of Edinburgh.

Chapter IV

1. *A Thousand Miles up the Nile*, p.86.
2. *Letters from Egypt* were first published in 1865. All quotations in this chapter are from the Virago Press edition of selections, 1983. A fuller edition, edited by Gordon Waterfield and containing more personal and political material, was published by Routledge in 1969. There is now a full-scale biography of Lucie Duff Gordon by Katherine Frank (Hamish Hamilton, London, 1994).
3. *A Thousand Miles up the Nile*, p.451.
4. Ibid, p.454.
5. Janet Ross's note to pp.84-5 of Lucie Duff Gordon's *Letters from Egypt*.
6. *A Thousand Miles up the Nile*, p.141.
7. Florence Nightingale's *Letters from Egypt*, p.77.
8. Ibid, p.176.
9. *A Thousand Miles up the Nile*, pp.115-16.
10. See *The Leisure of an Egyptian Official*, first published London, Hodder and Stoughton, 1921; published 1984 by Century Publishing, London, Hippocrene Books Inc., New York, Lester and Orpen Dennys Deneau, Ontario. Kenneth Rose in *The Later Cecils* (Weidenfeld and Nicolson, London, 1975) details Lord Edward's career in Egypt.
11. Admiration for her accuracy and range is enhanced by comparing her accounts with a standard and still readable work of the time, Edward W. Lane's *An account of the Manners and Customs of the Modern Egyptians*, 2 vols., Charles Knight and Company, London, 1837. Lane's sister, Mrs Sophia Poole, also wrote letters from Egypt, published as *The Englishwoman in Egypt* (Knight, London, 1844). She lacks Harriet Martineau's vigour of mind and Amelia Edwards's liveliness of style and she does not have the depth of thought of any of the three women with whom this book has been concerned; but her naiveté and her conscientiously plain unvarnished tale are endearing.

Bibliography

Arena, pp.299-310 (Boston, 1891),

British Library Additional Manuscripts, 45, 846 and 45, 847

Budge, Sir E.A. Wallis, *By Nile and Tigris*, Murray (London, 1920)

Carlyle, T., *Past and Present* (1843)

Cecil, Lord Edward, *The Leisure of an Egyptian Official*, Hodder and Stoughton (1921); Century Publishing (London), Hippocrene Books, Inc. (New York), Lester and Orpen Dennys Deneau (Ontario), (1984)

Christie, Agatha, *Death on the Nile* (1937); Fontana Books

Clayton, Peter A., *The Rediscovery of Ancient Egypt*, Thames and Hudson (1982, reprinted 1990)

Cook, Sir Edward, *The Life of Florence Nightingale*, 2 vols., Macmillan (London, 1913)

Cook, Thomas, *Up the Nile by Steam* (London, 1875-6)

David, Rosalie, *Macclesfield Collection of Egyptian Antiquities*, Aris and Phillips Ltd. (Warminster, 1980)

Drower, Margaret S., *Flinders Petrie* (London, 1985)

Duff Gordon, Lucie, *Letters from Egypt* (1865); ed. Gordon Waterfield, Routledge (London, 1969); Virago Press selections (1983)

Durrell, Lawrence, *The Alexandria Quartet*

Edwards, Amelia, *Hand and Glove*, Ward, Lock and Tyler (London, 1858)
Untrodden Peaks and Unfrequented Valleys (London, 1873)
A Thousand Miles up the Nile (1877); reprinted by Century (London, Sydney, Auckland, Johannesburg, 1984) and by Parkway and Darf (1993)
Pharoahs, Fellahs and Explorers, Osgood, Millvaine and Co. (London, 1891)

Elliott, Janice, *Life on the Nile*, Hodder and Stoughton (London, Sydney, Auckland, Toronto, 1989)

Forster, E.M., *A Passage to India* (1924)

Fowles, John, *Daniel Martin*, Jonathan Cape (London, 1977)

Frank, Katherine, *Lucie Duff Gordon*, Hamish Hamilton (London, 1994)

Golding, William, *The Scorpion God*, Faber (London, 1971)

Irby, C.L. and Mangles, J., *Travels in Egypt, Nubia, Syria and Asia Minor during the Years 1817 and 1818*, Darf Publishers Ltd (London, 1895)

Kinglake, A.W., *Eothen*, (1844); reprinted Macmillan (London, 1935)

Lane, E.W., *An Account of the Manners and Customs of the Modern Egyptians* 2 vols., Charles Knight and Co. (London, 1837)

Lear, Edward, *Selected Letters*, ed. Vivien Noakes, Clarendon Press (Oxford, 1988)

Martineau, Harriet, *Deerbrook* (1839); reprinted Virago (1983)

The Hour and the Man (1840)
Eastern Life Present and Past, Moxon (London, 1848)
Letters on the Laws of Man's Nature and Development (1850)
Autobiography, 2 vols., 1877; reprinted Virago (1983)
Murray, John, *A Handbook for Travellers in Egypt* (written by Sir G. Wilkinson) London, (1847)
Nightingale, Florence, *Letters from Egypt*, Spottiswood (London, 1854)
    Letters from Egypt: a Journey on the Nile, selected and introduced by Anthony Sattin, Barrie and Jenkins (London, 1987)
    Cassandra, Pickering and Chatto (London, 1991)
New England Magazine, The, vol. vii, no. 5, pp.548-64 (January, 1893)
North, Marianne, *Further Recollections of a Happy Life*, Macmillan (London, 1893)
Pemble, John, *The Mediterranean Passion*, Clarendon Press (Oxford, 1987)
Pichanik, Valerie, *Harriet Martineau*, University of Michigan Press (1980)
Poole, Mrs Sophia, *The Englishwoman in Egypt*, Knight (London, 1844)
Rose, Kenneth, *The Later Cecils*, Weidenfeld and Nicolson (London, 1975)
Saturday Review, The, April 23rd (1892)
Steegmuller, Francis, ed., *Flaubert in Egypt*, Bodley Head (London, Sydney, Toronto, 1972)
Strachey, Ray, *The Cause*, G. Bell and Sons (London, 1928)
Trollope, A., *The Bertrams*, (1859)
Warburton, Eliot, *The Crescent and the Cross*, (1844)
Winslow, William Copley, *The American Antiquarian*, XIV, No.6, pp.305-315 (November 1892)
Woodham-Smith, *Florence Nightingale, 1820-1910*, Constable (London, 1950)

Index

References to Harriet Martineau, Florence Nightingale and Amelia Edwards are indexed only when they occur outside the chapters devoted to these writers individually. Notes are indexed only when they contain material additional to that in the text.

Index of Places